# Sounds Like
# a Good Idea

**Also available from Network Continuum**

*Homo Zappiens* – Wim Veen and Ben Vrakking

*New Tools for Learning: Accelerated Learning meets ICT* – John Davitt

# Sounds Like a Good Idea

## Using audio technology in the classroom

## Mike Kinnaird

network
continuum

**Continuum International Publishing Group**

Network Continuum

The Tower Building                    80 Maiden Lane, Suite 704
11 York Road                          New York, NY 10038
SE1 7NX

www.networkcontinuum.co.uk
www.continuumbooks.com

**British Library Cataloguing-in-Publication Data**
A catalogue record for this book is available from the British Library.

ISBN: 9781855394483 (paperback)

**Library of Congress Cataloguing-in-Publication Data**
Kinnaird, Mike.
      Sounds like a good idea : using audio technology in the classroom / Mike Kinnaird.
         p.  cm.
      Includes index.
      ISBN 978-1-85539-448-3
   1.  Audio-visual education—United States. 2.  Radio in education—United States. 3.  Education
technology—United States.  I. Title.

      LB1044.2.K56 2008
      371.33'5—dc22

2008019547

Typeset by Ben Cracknell Studios | www.benstudios.co.uk
Printed and bound in Great Britain by Cromwell Press, Wiltshire

# Contents

# Foreword

## Are you taking the Mickey?

With media education finally beginning to gain the industrial credibility that has so long been sought after, it falls to practitioner-educators like Mike Kinnaird to move the training-education agenda to the next level, and this book will undoubtedly help in that challenge.

It has always seemed oxymoronic that critics chose the soubriquet 'Mickey Mouse', arguably the twentieth century's most successful iconic media creation, in an attempt to diminish the importance of media studies. That academics from diverse backgrounds spent most the latter part of the last century slugging it out for dominance in the emerging subject area, manifesting itself in some peculiar and nonsensical courses of study, is well documented. As recently as 2000, media educators were still being pilloried for offering degrees that lead inevitably to unemployment. Recent reports have generated data that corrects this rabid impression; for example, a BBC report in 2005 that trumpeted the fact that media students are among the most employable. We are better able to convey the emerging picture based upon the work now being undertaken by media educationalists in the UK.

With over 2.1 million jobs in the creative industries in the UK and the service sector growing consistently (as manufacturing declines further), university tutors have seen a further intriguing trend emerging. When being asked for references for graduates entering employment we are now no longer facing the question 'Are there jobs in the media?' but more 'Is there media in the job?'

Employers are reporting that media graduates are highly desired in the workplace for their wide-ranging skills-set, and that adaptability, ability to work as part of a team, and to find creative solutions are all prime factors in employment success today. The government's *Cox Review of Creativity In Business*, for example, has identified that all UK industry needs to enshrine creativity at the core of its activity if we are to challenge the development speed of America or Japan's economies.

At the University of Lincoln we have taken the challenge of educating the next generation of media practitioners very seriously indeed, a process contributed to by

Mike Kinnaird in his role as a visiting lecturer. Not only did the department start from the premise that a healthy mix of academics drawn from industry with those drawn from academia would strengthen the validity of the courses of study, but also that all research and developmental output by staff would be equally regarded. Along with world-ranking scholars publishing their seminal texts goes the broadcast and exhibition output that stimulates and validates our students' choice. It was only logical that being based in the ancient and media-neglected city of Lincoln that we would also address the issue of work-related issues, including output and distribution opportunities.

Together Mike and I worked on a unit of study that introduces students to the world of media-industry work, and encourages them to envision their future in relation to historical changes in the business. At times this unit both surprised and shocked us as it revealed astonishing mindsets alongside radical views about how the future will be, and what media will become. This study of the destination after their graduation has become a core part of the curriculum and is helping generate greater confidence in the students' minds.

In addition to a graduate business start-up centre, *Sparkhouse Studios*, and an in-house production arm, *Minerva Productions*, the use of short-term radio licences provided the radio students with an opportunity to reach a wider audience. Three-weekly licences per year were added to with *Ofcom's* permission, and gradually academics started experimenting with live-broadcast student assessments including material generated by students throughout the region. The next innovation encouraged final-year students to mentor small groups of schoolchildren to help them make their first radio show, never intervening to take over, but using every skill and tool in their arsenal learned on the programme to encourage and stimulate the youngsters to get a good show on air.

The success has been phenomenal. Bryan Rudd, the principal lecturer behind the initiative, has reported that students have demonstrated '. . . some inspired examples of prior learning adapted and incorporated into new and useful learning strategies'; headteachers, including Andrew Salmond Smith at St. Mary's Preparatory, Lincoln, have reported that their pupils have benefited: 'It was an exciting opportunity for a group of our Year 5 and Year 6 children to be given the chance to work together on their own radio programme, taking it from concept to finished article, guided and advised each step of the way by skilled undergraduates'; and *Ofcom* were moved to grant the first 24–7 community radio licence in the UK in recognition of the great work undertaken to literally give our young people and community groups 'a voice'. That it has fallen to education to provide industrial training can be seen in the growth in certainty around credible university offerings; and that education has simultaneously stepped into being a vital part of the distribution of social broadcasting is very significant. At a time when we talk of growth in peer-to-peer or one-to-few communication, at a time when traditional broadcast consumption among young people is falling steadily, to have found a third way of gluing communities together through regionalized education media outreach is very gratifying, and of immense importance to a geographically diverse region such as Lincolnshire.

Society is, however, still going about its vicious business; a survey of 200 students starting at Lincoln in Media Production in 2006 showed that 96 per cent of them had suffered someone making a negative comment to them when they announced they were going to university to study media. We must counter this outdated rhetoric, and the way to do this is through yet earlier education of pupils and their parents.

The Media Literacy campaign will help and the Creative and Media Diploma starting at age 15 will also help tackle this head-on. Schools and colleges with strong links to universities will be able to create viable and integrated development pathways that will ensure the best experience and practice of the media industry can be linked through all levels of education to eradicate doubt and dispel prejudice.

Mike Kinnaird's most useful book will shine a light on this pathway for all teachers and students at all stages and in all areas of the curriculum, leading to high-quality media practices; and those that practise them, becoming full and properly respected members of this society.

David Sleight
Head of Department, Media Production
University of Lincoln
November 2007

# Preface: One solution for the 21st century classroom

Tell me, and I will forget.
Show me, and I may remember.
Involve me, and I will understand.

*Confucius*, 450 BC

## The answer is yes; what was the question?

Audio will take you anywhere. You can be anyone, at any period of time in history; you can be the fifth Beatle or an evacuee in World War Two. You can motivate an audience, make them laugh and make them cry. You can make them buy something or you can tell them a story. As a platform of delivery you will lock into a lateral means of communication already explored in detail by your students in their private lives. You can record your thoughts, feelings and culture and share them with a class across time zones and continents within minutes by email.

You can build a radio station that mirrors industry or you can download free open-source audio-editing software that a 5 year old can use. You can start a project in an hour-long lesson and finish it. And what is more, it is perfectly possible to produce a product that sounds like the real thing; it sounds like a professional product we imagine we have heard somewhere else. So why do so many teachers, thrust sometimes not so willingly into the world of media technologies, opt for video as their first choice? Well, probably because no one has shown them what they can do with audio or how to do it.

Audio in the classroom is quick, simple and cost-effective. A teacher can make a complete audio project with a group in the time it takes to reboot the computer that has crashed for the umpteenth time under the weight of a gigantic video file.

Yes, of course video has a place and so does visual literacy. But there is no escaping the fact that video, even with today's kit, can be time-consuming and sadly hit and miss in the hands of inexperienced users. That is not a criticism, just a fact. It has disappointment built in. Unlike audio, it is also extremely difficult for a class to produce a video that looks the real deal. If you have doubts about that, just immerse yourself in *You Tube* for a while.

Young people are using audio like never before. Just when it seemed that radio was a dead duck and TV had finally ground it into the dirt, new and emerging technologies have changed the landscape. There are pockets of children's radio to be found on the internet, although large numbers of so called children's radio sourced by search engines often turns out to be college radio instead. The UK, for so many years the flag-bearers of public service broadcasting, has little to be proud of in this area. All major radio broadcasters in the UK have wiped their hands of children's radio. With a microscope you will find *CBeebies* on BBC7, a digital channel tucked away in the dark recess of DAB radio or digital television boxes. And that is presuming you knew that in the first place, because neither the BBC nor commercial radio has any taste for encouraging children to listen to the radio with parents as they did even 20 years ago. There are reasons of course: commercial radio has horns locked over sponsors and advertising as the market fragments and splinters all over the place; and advertisers available in local areas may not be interested in a children's audience.

I can't imagine the story is different now in any country you care to mention. Even in the 1980s, an established DJ friend of mine had his children's show abruptly scrapped at a northern commercial station when a new sponsor took over the slot. Not many 12 year olds buy beds apparently, so the programme went. But what is the BBC's excuse? Let's not use small audiences as a reason when digital television platforms are happy with adult network audiences measured in hundreds of thousands. It is a sad situation.

'Across the curriculum, radio can be used to inspire students, it's that simple': the opening comment from Dr Guy Starkey during our conversation (see Chapter 8). Guy is Acting Associate Dean (Media) at the University of Sunderland. He is also one of the UK's leading radio academics. I spoke to him and others while writing this book and, to be honest, the song remains the same, regardless to whom I spoke.

Audio will help you, as teacher, to take the curriculum to new areas. Not only will it help bring some subjects alive, it will introduce some teachers to a platform already understood by the majority of students in the class.

As Professor John West-Burnham points out: 'If you look at the way young people live their lives, they are incredibly media-rich.'

In his case study featured in this book (see Chapter 11), John outlines his views on the use of audio in the classroom. The central theme to his argument is that young people already have sophisticated personal tools and networks at their disposal and can take full advantage of media practices when introduced into the curriculum: 'It's what the Dutch call homo-zapiens. Young people can communicate with each other in numerous ways and often simultaneously.'

In this book we will explore how others have used audio in the past. We will discuss equipment needs and outline what to buy and, crucially, what not to buy. A top tip from the start: do not spend thousands of pounds on acoustic treatment in your designated classroom cum radio studio when old blankets and a selection of egg boxes will do the job. From school radio stations to audio in a geography class and from primary to secondary classes, we consider ideas that are easily achieved, quick and cheap to produce.

We will look at some figures in a moment but, for now, we should realize that in spite of the way radio as an industry in particular has treated them, young people use audio for information, communication and entertainment. If we ignore that then maybe we are missing a trick here. Audio is a viable and realistic means of not only bonding within a school but also a tricky bit of bridging the gap to the community, and sharing experiences and learning with that community.

Your students will already have some skills and understanding and are increasingly used to accessing audio information on demand. They are using a variety of platforms to do this from mobile phones to podcasts and listen-again audio. So why do some schools ban mobile phones and others positively embrace them? During a recent short-term FM radio broadcast I worked on at a school, students spent their lunchtime listening to the output on their phones. Is that not a clue?

Young people are leading the way and if we do not follow as a partnership, then should we be surprised at the numbers of students who feel no one is talking their language? Thankfully, audio can at least provide some solutions. The latest figures at time of writing suggest that the number of 15 year olds in the UK who listened to the radio via their mobile phone during 2006/7 rose by 27 per cent to 4.4 million, with 1.8 million of those aged between 15 and 24. Again, in 2007, one in eight people listened regularly to their favourite shows on a digital platform; that will only increase. Listening to digital-only radio stations jumped markedly from 905,000 in 2003 to 6.09 million in 2007; podcasts are clearly gaining, with 2.7 million listeners over the age of 15, an increase from just under 2 million in 2006.

This book then is about audio with some ideas on how to use it. It is for teachers of anything you like, not just media; teachers of secondary-age students or of primary classes, maybe colleges too. The reason is simple: audio when used to its best advantage is the most extraordinary tool.

In this book, you will find some examples of how that has been done, along with some examples of how you can use audio in all manner of subject areas, from geography to sports studies to modern foreign languages. You will see how citizenship and PSHE, rarely the number one choice of the average pupil, can be turned around, and how audio can create a bridge between the school and community, creating genuine extended learning opportunities.

All it needs is a little creativity and the willingness to try new skills and share those skills with others; a willingness to adopt a partnership with your pupils who will use some of the techniques in this book in their private lives anyway, as masters of the download and MP3.

You will find examples among the case studies of radio projects and how your school can run your own FM radio station with far-reaching, successful consequences; you will come across some ideas for equipment (although bear in mind that technology changes faster than ever before so what is here is only a guide). There are hints on recording and interview techniques, and anecdotes from my previous 20-year career in broadcasting to illustrate that not everything goes according to plan every time, such as the incomprehensible interview recorded inside a seaside hotel that was being demolished and why that was a turning point in my understanding of audio, and the occasions when I got to the end of a recording only to find I had not put a tape in the machine in the first place. To err is human, as they say.

Audio works just as well as an individual project as a group project – audio diaries, jingles, radio commercials, full radio programmes, a sports commentary, a children's story in German, an audio book for primary children, a descriptive account in geography of what happened when that volcano blew – the development of some highly sophisticated communication skills without the reliance of visual images; speaking and listening to the fore.

Figures aside, the fact remains that radio in its various guises is enjoying good times and the predictions chanted by some that young people are abandoning radio are almost certainly wrong. It is just that they are using audio in different ways in their private lives and it is now they who are driving the content and the agenda. If we are not adopting their means of communication then maybe we should not be too surprised that they no longer see the relevance in what we have to offer.

There are exciting times ahead in the twenty-first century classroom. Just press record.

# Acknowledgments

Without John West-Burnham there would be no book. My grateful thanks for his constant support and suggesting there was a need to champion the cause. To David Sleight for endless encouragement and to all the case study contributors who agreed to be interviewed when they were all busy. Lastly, a huge thank you to my family who lost me to a laptop for six months.

# Introduction

## Using audio to engage students

All I can say after more than 20 years in broadcasting, followed by a new career in teaching and training, is that media technologies work in the classroom. We all know that video is a chosen favourite in schools but audio can offer a sensible alternative that is often cheaper and faster to turn around. This book is intended to be a guide and celebration of audio; how to create audio projects and offer some thoughts on how audio can be used across the curriculum.

As well as celebrating success, the idea of the book is to illustrate some pitfalls and to look at projects that have not always gone according to plan.

Dip in and out of the book; take note of help in the recording and edit sections, the lesson ideas, and enjoy some of the past experiences featured in the case studies.

It is worth spending a little time reflecting on the deeper understanding, benefits and background to the use of audio as a concept.

Perhaps the starting point should be the briefest look at John Reith, the first Director General of the BBC in 1922. After being Director General for just a year or so, he invited the Archbishop of Canterbury and his wife around to dinner. There weren't many radio sets in homes, so the Archbishop was invited to listen. The radio in the dining room was switched on, and this caused a great deal of surprise to the Archbishop and his wife who said she was astonished that the radio waves could travel through the windows. Apparently she was expecting to open the windows so that the radio waves could be let in. It is very difficult now to appreciate the scale of what was happening in the early years of the twentieth century.

Radio as entertainment and information was an adaptation of a military purpose. The technical trick was to enable one person to talk to another over distances. It took visionaries like the young Scottish engineer, John Reith, to see a potential far beyond that. Of course we had the chicken and egg situation so common even today. Manufacturers had produced equipment capable of listening to a signal, but had nothing to broadcast. Someone, somewhere, had to decide what to do with the idea; create programmes – whatever they were.

The British establishment, with its predictable reserve and inherent need to maintain its authority, made certain that the masses were given a wholesome diet of carefully chosen materials and nothing else. What they did not want at any price was people thinking that radio could be used for raucous entertainment and general frivolity. Certainly not. A view thoroughly endorsed by the towering, church-minded Reith who served programmes rich in sermon, quality classical music and readings.

The stiff-collared British could only watch in despair as the Americans not only embraced radio, but positively encouraged an explosion of stations as soon as technically possible, entertaining listeners as they went. The British were having none of that nonsense and held out for decades, successfully bypassing rock 'n' roll, only caving in to public demand following the unstoppable success of pirate radio that blasted away from converted trawlers and wartime forts off the coast.

The thought that mere members of the public could ever take part in such projects was beyond imagination at the time. This, remember, is the days when the only way to get a request on the radio was to send a postcard or a letter. It was, of course, until recent years a shared family experience. We certainly don't sit around the radio set any more like the Archbishop's wife.

What has changed now is that we can take part in every sense, and schools can create their own programming. Technology, and its cost, has changed so dramatically in recent years that there is every opportunity for schools to harness the development of radio and create their own radio stations, not just around school, but around their communities with an RSL (restricted service licence) broadcasting on FM.

The following pages of this section outline how a school can develop a radio station, either in the school as an internal service or, at the other extreme, as an FM radio station which broadcasts to the wider community on a short-term licence.

There is one inescapable fact that will be ignored at our peril. Our children live in a world swamped with media input and influences, and yet I am not the first to publish the suggestion that there are plenty of those in education who would prefer not to recognize that and pretend instead that it does not happen. And those people remain surprised that their carefully constructed timetable fails to connect with children from a huge range of cultural, social and family backgrounds. If we are to have any realistic hope of delivering education to twenty-first century children, then we have to open our eyes to the delivery platforms available and, in particular, to the platforms that children recognize, use, employ and disseminate among themselves. This has to be, if we are to have the slightest chance of providing a curriculum that is relevant to children's lives.

Mobile phones are a case in point. A leading academic I spoke to reminded me of a conference for headteachers that he attended. One headteacher said he had recently banned all students and staff from having mobile phones in school because they were a distraction and a continuous nuisance. Another headteacher, sitting at the same table, piped up that he had just insisted that every student must have a mobile phone because it provided him with instant communication. Such polar-opposite views are bound to happen but that is little comfort when attempting to unravel what will actually benefit the children.

This is the Playstation/X-Box generation used to quick fixes of information. In many cases we are currently not addressing the need of this generation, but sticking to a method of giving information in a way that seems foreign, distant and irrelevant. This is as relevant to the under-12s as to the graduates. Why continue with a classroom structure more suited to the nineteenth or twentieth century than the twenty-first?

Even at its most basic and simplistic level, what I suggest is a method of teaching, training and learning that is enjoyable, that is fun to do and to take part in. The National Curriculum in England and Wales, it could be argued, has been particularly successful in stripping fun out of just about everything, replacing it with targets and something or other that must be qualified, quantified and fitted for processing in a league table. Of course it is not one size fits all. There will be students who remain unsure, shy of taking part or still see it as just another lesson – but that should not stop us from trying.

Away from the curriculum, it is certainly possible to introduce self-confidence and speaking and listening to many students who lack even the most basic attributes. Bright school leavers are not getting the jobs they want because they lack speaking skills at interviews. And that is not just me making these noises: a UK government report suggested that verbal communication should be a major part of literacy – that these were not soft skills, as previously widely suggested, but vital skills for today's students.

Well, of course, there is nothing wrong with the pencil. It is a perfectly acceptable way to communicate with someone else, and perfectly suited to many children. But this determination in education to close the door fails to recognize that the world beyond the classroom has moved on, that values and expectations have changed and that mass communication methods and skills are changing faster than at any time in our history. Countless children now operate in a different world; they have different views and use a language alien to many adults. They have advance social-networking skills that can operate on different levels simultaneously.

The wheel has been invented now so this book is, I hope, just one small attempt to embrace that. That does not mean to say that we accept all the shortcomings and do not strive to find some quality control in there; this is not meant to be a free-for-all. What I am suggesting is that we look at how the rest of the world connects with our children, build in our own quality threshold and look at how we can practically use emerging technology, train teachers accordingly, and find ways of funding some of that development. In many cases it will be a subtle shift here and there in a lesson; in others it will be a huge cultural shift.

Whatever the shift, it will be relevant to the future working lives of children and will go some way to enable schools to bond with their own internal and external communities, becoming extended learning experiences rather than simply extended schools. Audio is not the be-all and end-all, but it is one proven means of breaking down barriers between students, of integrating cultures, of recognizing and respecting contributions. School radio can very quickly create a sense of pride and belonging and a widespread sense of identity. Some successful schools though will see audio projects – radio or otherwise – as an opportunity to connect with the wider community; an opportunity to involve as many stakeholders as possible in creating educational opportunities and experiences, of linking schools and families, with a shared ownership of what is taking place and of any outcomes.

# Part 1

## Recording, editing and basic mixing techniques

# 1 Putting audio into context

In this chapter we consider the overall place for audio in the classroom and its role as a means of bridging and connecting with the wider community. Audio and school radio in particular will be considered as a tool toward the delivery of *Every Child Matters* and personalization. This chapter also looks at creating a school identity and, crucially, an identity and sense of purpose for the community. We look at some of the key points in setting up a school radio service, particularly the short-term FM licence – there are plenty of ideas of how to use school radio in simpler forms in curriculum subject areas in Part 2 of this book. Finally there is brief introduction to the basics of audio equipment (see chapters 2 and 7 for more details on this).

## The school, the radio and the community

Schools are not territories but communities and shared resources collectively owned. At least, they should be. Respect for resources should be a basic requirement and that includes the product as well as the equipment.

Using audio in the classroom, such as radio, takes on another dimension that requires respect on all sides, for equipment as well as judgements, attitudes, responses, even gut feelings. The most obvious difference of using audio on this scale is that the end product is likely to be shared and witnessed by a large number of people and it can involve a fairly large group of people to produce it. We all like some radio stations but not all presenters; we've become button-pushers in radio the same way that we channel-hop our television stations. We are no longer so keen to stay with one station all day, everyday. In short, we are all different and what I like, you may well not like. So respecting the opinion of others on radio projects is an important point, particularly when teachers and students attempt jointly to make progress. The wise head of the teacher, built on personal experiences, needs to be balanced with the young student who often talks in a different language and understands their own market.

This respect should also extend to a wider respect for the community beyond. There is a real opportunity with radio to forge links, mend fences and to integrate students with sections of their community with whom they would never normally interact. See page 44 for examples on how students can record (and use as programme items) various community groups such as the single-parent group. There is a real chance here for the school radio project to reflect not only what the community is about, but also to lead, influence, share experiences and meet social exclusion and low self-esteem head on. This may all sound rather grand and somewhat ambitious but how many times though have we seen again and again students, and indeed families, with little or no ambition?

For many years, I have lived and worked in a quiet rural community with non-higher education families and with a well-established family history of working in agriculture. Year by year, bit by bit, that industry had all but disintegrated with machines taking the place of considerable numbers of men. Although these families are better connected in some ways, in that some have reasonable access to their own transport, they still remain within themselves, expecting nothing and, generally speaking, getting nothing by return. The community is characterized by modest housing, poor recreational facilities, low wages, seasonal work, abysmal public transport and limited access to any further education opportunities. It's an area dominated for generations by weekly newspapers where something that happened last Tuesday is big news. An area, where even now, there's a serious need to address lifelong learning and how people are supposed to access it when there is not even a bus to take them, should they be able to afford it or find the motivation. It's an area where media outlets are still thin on the ground even though the weekly papers are now feeling the squeeze experienced elsewhere. People here are dependent on their families but also on agencies to support their needs, agencies that still operate, it could be argued, within the silo system, working independently.

Radio projects can hit England's *Every Child Matters* initiative square-on and provide an opportunity for agencies to move from silo to service, the joined-up thinking approach much talked of in recent times. Certainly, community radio, the government's planned 'third tier' of radio, offers an unprecedented opportunity to meet these needs; schools, colleges and universities have a real chance to engage with and indeed lead such schemes. This is something we will look at in general terms in this chapter.

We know that low social class, poverty, dysfunctional families and a community of low social capital can have a profound effect on educational achievement. So *Every Child Matters* is there to prevent the problem rather than fix it. If we accept that no school alone can meet all the needs of *Every Child Matters*, then audio, as radio and other forms discussed elsewhere, can go a long way to challenging it.

How straightforward it is to cover the key outcomes of *Every Child Matters – Being healthy, Staying safe, Enjoying and achieving, Making a positive contribution* and *Achieving economic well-being*.

Record a piece with a local dietician, vox pop students in the street on eating habits, challenge a local café to produce healthy menus. Edit and package together for a two-minute audio feature. Follow that up by taking a detailed look at one typical family, what food they buy and why, noting how cost and the cooking skills within the family play a part in decisions. How influential are the children in the family determining what they will or will not eat? How strict are parents in insisting children eat a balanced diet and sit at a table rather than the games console? Is eating a shared or solitary experience characterized by what can be grabbed from the freezer? How does a lack of transport affect choice when it comes to food buying?

Is this not *Every Child Matters*?

Students collect prizes from local retailers for competitions they plan to run. They must negotiate and get as many 'freebies' as possible, being aware that the retailer is not handing over profits simply for the student to give away but persuading the retailer that there really is something in it for them. They negotiate placing a poster advertising their school radio station in a shop window, persuade the manager to record a brief jingle or ident (identity) for the station on the spot, maybe even sponsor an event associated with the station's launch. Entrepreneurial skills surely?

Creating a radio project that in itself embraces tolerance and respect, shares in social learning and provides services to the wider community is certainly part of the *Every Child Matters* initiative. The exercise has little to do with the curriculum perhaps, and does not always fit neatly into the rigid categories of subject areas, but does that have to be the criteria every single time? Is this not about the rounded development of the student with an eye to what happens next when they leave the fur-lined comfort zone of school or college? Does it not benefit the student? Is there not a long-term gain to be won here? Would this not benefit those students who do feel that school is a random series of hour-long subjects in which they see little relevance? Would projects such as these not give some families a sense that they do have a relevant part to play after all; something that parents can identify with and talk to their children about?

# School radio, broadcasting on FM

## A Restricted Service Licence

School radio is becoming more and more popular. Schools can apply, like anyone else, for an FM radio broadcast licence. Hospital radio stations have been doing it for years and many local events such as agricultural shows or festivals frequently do so. Yes, it is expensive but the rewards for schools, if done properly, can be enormous. Just make sure you go in with your eyes open because this cannot be set up in a couple of weeks; and you do need some support to make sure preparations are in hand.

This is rightly seen as the high-end use of audio within the classroom and should not be attempted lightly (there are more straightforward examples of audio elsewhere in the book, see Chapter 5). If done correctly, an RSL (restricted service licence on FM) is a huge and highly-effective marketing tool for any school or college. If done badly, it could be a public relations disaster.

So to go back a bit, what is an RSL? In a nutshell, it is a licence to broadcast within a small area, for no more than 28 consecutive days a year. You can have no more than two licences, four months apart in any calendar year (one licence if you are within the M25). There are a couple of exceptions to the 28-day rule: it is possible to broadcast on AM for a series of events or within a very confined space, such as a stadium, on very low FM power. Frankly, that's no real benefit to schools so we will move on.

A few simple points to start with. No, you cannot simply throw up an aerial and start broadcasting whenever you feel like it. It's a process overseen by *Ofcom* in the UK, the independent broadcast regulator that keeps an eye on everything from commercial radio and television misdemeanours to mobile phone technologies. You need *Ofcom*'s permission to do anything, and what it says goes; there are no shortcuts. If it says you can't, you can't. However, don't be put off at this stage; it's likely that a school will get permission as long as a few simple guidelines are followed. Teachers can apply and the only real relevant restriction is that licences are not granted to anyone who has previously been refused a licence or who has a conviction for illegal broadcasting.

There are two basic types of RSL:

- the short-term licence which runs for a continuous period – for example, a week or two weeks at the end of the summer term or around Christmas.
- the long-term licence, where broadcasts are either made on separate days or are at very low power, as in the case of hospitals and colleges which transmit to that site only.

The short-term RSL may be allowed up to a 25-watt transmitter which could take a signal for quite some distance around a town, even beyond a small market town and into surrounding villages. It can depend on what is in the way of that signal, how high the aerial is and weather conditions. In the summer, for example, high pressure sucks the signal up and away and it does not travel so far; low pressure with low clouds can bounce the signal down a bit and travel some distance. Sound waves and transmitters have no respect for neat boundaries so it is impossible to say how far a signal will travel.

Many years ago, I was producing an outside broadcast for a local radio station in a small market town that sat in a natural dip. It was a challenge transmitting from there with equipment which was not as sophisticated as today's. All looked perfect on a glorious summer's day with soaring temperatures. That is when it all went horribly wrong. The two engineers with me at the time could only stare at the transmitting vehicle as the signal abruptly disappeared half way through the programme. Silence. I was talking but no one more than six feet away would ever know. It was left to a technician back in the studio to hurriedly wake up and find a record, as it was back then, to fill in the gaps. There was nothing to do until the weather stopped being so unreasonably cheerful and got back to its usual English mood.

*Ofcom* will certainly keep an eye on your transmitter and will check to make sure you have not adjusted it to boost that signal still more. It was not unheard of for the school RSLs I have been involved with to achieve a distance of 12 to 15 miles from the studio – and that was with a fairly low aerial.

For a normal short-term RSL, complete a form on the *Ofcom* website and send two copies (plus a map of the broadcast area) with an application fee of £400 to the regulator, a minimum of six weeks before the broadcast is planned to start. No fee – no licence: that six-week rule is important to note. *Ofcom* will not register or process your application until the application fee is received. On top of that there is a £40 per day Wireless Telegraphy Act licence fee (the government basically) to use an allocated piece of the FM band, plus £30 per day which goes to *Ofcom*. These fees and the application fee are zero-rated for VAT. Again, do not take chances. These fees must be paid up front otherwise no licence. Without a licence, the school or college would be committing an offence if caught broadcasting.

You will have gathered that nothing is free but, when it comes to music, that always surprises people. There is a widespread assumption that playing tunes on the radio costs nothing. Wrong, I'm afraid.

Years ago working in BBC local radio, we had to complete paper forms, writing down every single detail; name of the artist, composer, publisher, label, arranger, the prefix and suffix numbers and the precise duration of the song we played. And that was for every song. Independent listeners would be out there recording our output as spot-checks, like secret shoppers, double-checking our music logs and woe betide those who did not complete their logs in time or miss out a tune. Simply, it was for payment purposes. If you played four seconds of this and five seconds of that in a programme trail, then that is what you logged.

Now, thank heavens, the system is somewhat simpler. Computers automatically log music in most radio stations. As far as we are concerned here, royalties to the three main music organizations are needed if the school intends to broadcast any commercially available music. At the time of writing it is £31.85 per day (if paid in advance) for the PRS (Performing Rights Society) author/composer royalty licence; £35 per day for the PPL artist/performer royalty licence; the MCPS production music/recording copyright licence per 28 days for an audience of up to 100,000 if paid in advance is £54. So if a school were to consider a full 28-day licence, the operating fees stand at around £5000. Basically it's not cheap, hence the week at the end of a term becomes quite attractive and frankly, more manageable. Funding streams are an obvious answer and in fact every school RSL I have been part of has been funded externally.

So, to equipment. Many schools are now investing in radio studios of their own with varying success. Some are buying equipment they will never use and others not considering additional needs such as acoustics.

A room with clear hard walls will have its share of echo and reverb that will spoil the sound. There is plenty of advice about this in Chapter 7. However, one cheap and effective option to damp down that echo can be achieved with thick, heavy curtains hung directly on the wall. The fabric will soak up any additional 'bounce' from the sound.

Maybe buying a multi-channel sound desk and rack-mounted CD players are not an option right now. If buying equipment for a permanent studio is not desirable or an option at this stage, then there are companies who can hire you kit for the purpose. Alternatively, check if there's an existing RSL near you – that hospital radio station or football stadium that already has equipment and is currently not in use. They may well hire to you at favourable rates or even offer for free. You will, of course, need to know how to get the sound from your studio to the transmitter and aerial but a hire company will be able to offer advice. Essentially, the output of the studio must connect to a transmitter, and a cable attached to the transmitter goes to the aerial or 'mast'.

Don't even think about buying a transmitter, the costs are enormous. *Ofcom* can supply you with a list of reputable transmitter engineers around the country who will hire what you need. *Ofcom* will tell you what FM frequency you have been allocated when it issues you with a licence. Clearly if the school is in a large metropolitan area awash with radio competition, then the frequency choice will be a tight squeeze on the available band. It will also tell you how powerful the transmitter can be – for example, 25 watts. Those details then go to the transmitter supplier who programmes the transmitter; you should also be able to hire the necessary cabling and an appropriate aerial from this same company.

Don't take any shortcuts at this stage. The technical bit has to be spot on. You will get an on-site visit from *Ofcom* engineers who will check the transmitter and that you are doing what you said you would in your application. During the last RSL I worked on, at Monks' Dyke Technology College in Louth with Robin Webber-Jones, engineers told me they had closed down two broadcasts in recent weeks because the equipment was not up to scratch. *Ofcom* will take you off the air and has the power to confiscate equipment. Deal with reputable companies and listen to advice. Ask *Ofcom* if you're not sure.

# Audio equipment

## Testing, testing . . .

First point to note: there is no such thing as the best microphone.

Time and again I am asked which is the best microphone and it is an almost impossible question to answer. Almost, in that everyone has a favourite for a multitude of reasons, and I could not give a direct answer until I had more information to hand.

The microphone is obviously at the heart of what you are hoping to achieve. It is what will record the sound you are looking for. As to prices, you can pay what you want to pay, from next to nothing to thousands of pounds. The reason why I am saying that I do not know the best microphone for you is because I do not know what you want it for. Is this high-end musical recording or simply, as with most people who will pick up this book, to record a voice to a reasonable standard?

At this point can I plead for some common sense? Equipment suppliers will naturally want you to spend money and a quick trawl through search engines will swamp you with products. Bear in mind most of that information is directed at musicians and those looking for good to high quality recording and may not be what you need. Ten or fifteen years ago £200 was a sensible sum to spend on a good microphone, whereas now £50 will be more than adequate. Prices have changed that much. The important point to bear in mind is your budget because you know what you can spend. So, do we buy a first rate *AKG*, *Sennheiser* or *Beyer* mic (microphone) or a £1 or £10 mic from the supermarket? All those manufacturers make superb industry standard microphones of the highest quality and I have used some from each of those and many others too. However, does it follow that the £10 microphone from the supermarket or budget high street shop should automatically be disregarded?

I have used a £10 microphone plugged into my PC at home to record presentations with *Windows Moviemaker* that I showed to students. Not once did a student say that they enjoyed the presentation but frankly the frequency response on the microphone left something to be desired. They do not notice and could not care less: it is what I said, how I said it, and the overall product I created that counted. The only addition I used was to wrap a piece of foam from an old thrown-out chair around the business end of the microphone, as a windshield – not perfect but it worked well.

Media professionals are still coming to terms with the fact that the benchmark of quality that has been a cornerstone of media production for many years is not necessarily the benchmark for the next generation reared on internet, home-produced content.

I trained in an industry where nothing less than perfect was acceptable. That does not mean that we should let standards slip or we should stop striving for the very best quality every time. It just means that sometimes we need to be realistic.

What do you want the microphone for? Who will use it? How will it be used? Is a superb sound quality critical to the end result or is it a means of recording some words? A fantastic microphone but hopeless speakers will still leave you with a muffled mess. If your recording is focused on clarity of pronunciation and intonation, then spending more may be the only option.

If you want 25 mics to plug into computers in your class that will be used by a group of 10 or 14 year olds, would you want to spend £50 a time even if you could? The answer I think is obvious.

If you are creating a radio studio in your school, then expensive high quality microphones with good headphones and speakers, or monitors as they tend to be called in studios, are not just desirable but essential. Everything depends on what it is you are trying to achieve.

There are more details in Chapter 2 and in Peter Knowles' case study in Chapter 7.

# 2 Basic recording techniques

This chapter takes a detailed look at how the absolute beginner can record and process their audio. There are key tips and hints on how to produce the best recordings possible, regardless of the situation, as well as suggestions on how to avoid mistakes that can ruin all that hard work, and why a pair of old curtains could shave hundreds of pounds from the school's audio acoustic treatment bill.

The main points featured in this chapter are:

- Before you start, make sure you know what you want to achieve
- Write scripts in the spoken not written word
- Buying headphones
- How to avoid mic rattle noises
- Advice on where and where not to record, and simple tips on how to avoid reverb
- How to hold a microphone to avoid mic-popping sounds when your breath hits the mic
- The importance of good speakers in a school radio studio when monitoring a programme or editing.

## How to record audio

### Stop before you start

Now we are getting to the nitty gritty. Time to roll up the sleeves and get something recorded. Except, perhaps I should call this 'how not to record' from the very start.

Before you even think about recording anything, before you plug a microphone in, before you get the recorder out of the cupboard, there are a few things to sort out. This is straightforward enough and should not cause unlimited headaches if you think through these few basics.

I will mention at this point that the occasional minor snag, bordering on potential disaster, can be rescued at the editing stage, but it is best not to rely on that, so let's try to record fault-free from the beginning.

From the days when we manhandled huge reel-to-reel tape machines around to today as we saunter around using digital recorders, the principles remain the same. Before you do anything, make sure you know what it is you want to record. What exactly are you trying to achieve?

Microphones are clever bits of kit but they cannot work it out for you and they can only do what they can do. So first things first: who and what are we recording and where are we doing it? Do we have a script or is this off the cuff? Do those recording know what to expect?

Let me give you an example. There have been times when I have been asked to record a piece of drama. Not a problem if all the players – and let's hope there is not many of them – are all in a confined and reasonably small space. Sadly no. You find there is a stage full and they are all performing the play for real, leaping about here and there, with people speaking from opposite wings of the stage. Well, unless you are nifty on you toes and can find a way of keeping all the rattling of equipment and your increasingly breathless condition to a minimum, and you can second guess where the next dialogue is coming from, then you have not got a chance. Forget it.

Equally, there have been times when students arrive with scraps of paper that may or may not have once been scripts, to record a piece for a geography or English project. With the finger poised over a record button, it then transpires that no one has a clue who is saying what or when, or if anyone has even read the words out loud beforehand. Banana skins abound.

So to go back to the beginning, know what it is you want to do and achieve first.

If you are using a script, do those taking part know their individual parts and does it all make sense? Read scripts aloud. Call it rehearsal if that makes everyone feel better because this can be unsettling for some. As a rule, we do not read aloud and have not done so since primary school days, or we often avoid reading in class if at all possible. We become very aware of our voices or in some cases very aware of how much we struggle over certain words and phrases. This can be embarrassing and have a detrimental impact on some students' self-confidence.

I read news scripts for many, many years in my previous broadcasting career, live and recorded. The same rules applied then. Only a complete idiot or the gloriously self-confident ever go near a microphone without reading the words beforehand. On very rare occasions, of course, that is not always possible so there is an element of fingers crossed. However, even after 20 years of professional work, I would not wish to read a script without testing it out. We all have tricky words that just never seem to come out right or a combination of words that set out to make our life awkward. Reading the sports bulletins during Wimbledon week, with half the players' surnames a mass of anagrams and a creative use of Z and Y, still makes my palms sweat with sheer nerves.

An important point to note here. Stick to the spoken word whenever writing a script that is clearly meant to be that person talking. The spoken word is not the same as the written word.

The spoken word enables us to break all the rules, so we can write *can't, shan't, won't* and *don't* because that's how we speak. It is a conversational style, or a narrative if you prefer, and clearly some people find it harder than others. Experience shows that younger students, from the text generation, find this informality far easier than their teachers.

Another simple point to bear in mind is that we tend to speak in short sentences. Don't we? Yes, we do. Fine. So write as you speak, and the intended audience is more likely to keep up. You can try ad-libbing but be prepared for numerous 'takes' and plenty of time editing – it is a skill that will prove very useful later but, for now, let us not complicate matters.

So a lesson learned. Read it and make sure you are confident. If not, change it or swap with someone else. (Interviews are a little different and there is more on this in Chapter 4.) Make sure what you want to record can be practically achieved. Editing can help later, but it is best not to rely on that.

So are you recording in a lively, echoey room? Classrooms are often characterized by square hard walls. Recording can pick up more than a little reverb from the room, making it sound as though you are in the basement. It is not an attractive sound. Corridors and offices can be equally awkward. One way of checking is simply to clap your hands or click your fingers. You will be able to hear any tail off from the sound. If you can hear those, then so will the microphone.

One way of avoiding that is to huddle in a corner. The closeness of the walls as a V shape can help absorb some of that bounce from the sound. Use heavy curtains or old blankets on the walls to soften the sound.

All rules are there to be broken of course and there could be times when that natural reverb works for you. For example, you may be recording a sporting activity in a sports hall or gym, perhaps as a sound effect or the mock-up of a sports commentary. In that case the reverb is exactly what you want because it helps tell the story of where you are. It would not be the same without the reverb because I can see in my in my mind's eye exactly where the recording is taking place; I do not even need to tell the audience where I am. Recording in a suitable location can be a significant bonus in telling a story.

There were endless occasions where I would go to record an interviewee on location only to be directed to the quietest room possible away from the action. That is quite understandable because it is a natural assumption that people make. They believe that if you want to record something, keep out any background sound. But remember, sound is what we are about. We are about engaging students, giving them something to spark their senses, keeping them with us as long as possible, so give them something to hang their ears on. The 'quiet room offer' was made to me once when visiting a knitwear factory. The sound on the workroom floor was gigantic, a cacophony of knitting machines, sewing machines snarling and growling with the occasional bellowed instruction, even a radio struggling and failing to make itself heard over the top. But close your eyes, listen and imagine where else could you be. The sound told the story. I did not need to say where I was because the listener could hear it illustrated perfectly by the sound.

So for example, let us assume you are recording a food technology exercise. This exercise may be available as an audio recipe for students who find keeping up a little tricky and are not confident about writing accurate details from the board. So the audio file is there just as a back-up or a means of introducing a different approach as a lesson starter. If that is the case, record that example in the school or college food technology rooms along with the clattering pans. Plenty of sounds spring to mind; foods frying in a pan, taps turned on to fill a pan, cans opened, aluminium foil ripped from the box and of course the delighted murmurs from the testers after the event. If this means the teacher being recorded goes off-mic on occasion to get something, then so much the better (just don't make a habit of it). It will only help to give a sense of physical space to the recording and add to the illustration.

This point goes back to earlier points about thinking the piece through first and what it is you are trying to achieve. Recording this way is a simple means of providing an engaging starter. The experiment, experience or project can be briefly recorded in advance and played back to the class or saved in a computer drive as a reminder.

## Begin recording

For the sake of example, we will assume at this stage that you are using a portable recording device of some description. Different books will give different advice on what to do next but many will say hold the microphone nine inches away from your guest's mouth, an instruction I have even seen further education lecturers hand out without any thought whatsoever. Nonsense. How you record and from what distance will depend on numerous factors if you want to get the best possible sound.

How far the microphone should be from your mouth or anyone else's will depend at the very least on the room that you are recording in and how loud those voices are. To state the obvious, if the person you are recording has a large booming voice the mic will need to be further away than the small, quiet, very young voice. If that room has natural reverb then placing the microphone a little closer than seems normal will go some way to helping.

If you really want some guidance on this, then extend your little finger and thumb outstretched. The distance between the tip of the finger and the thumb can be the distance between your mouth and the mic. But please use this as a guide only – not a rule. Always listen first.

Modern technology that is commonplace in many classrooms can conspire against us. Computers can issue a hum that microphones pick up, so recording in a computer room can prove a challenge. More than one recording of mine in the past has fallen foul to the fluorescent strip light and of course it's always when you listen back that the problem becomes apparent. Those lights often make themselves known with a buzz that sits in the background of the recording so it is a good idea not to record directly underneath.

Your recording device may have an automatic recording level. In other words the equipment listens to the recording and adjusts the levels for you, so you don't have to worry about distortion. It's a bit like the automatic gearbox of a car – push into forward, put your foot down and away it goes.

However, the recording device may require that you set the record volume levels yourself. It is a good idea, in that case, to test the recording first. Voice levels often change when the mic is switched on. People either talk more quietly or loudly, depending on how much nerves kick in; either way, that can be a problem for obvious reasons. So do a dummy run, stop, and listen to what you have got. It can save considerable time. However, you will need to watch record levels on occasion throughout the recording to make sure those levels are still OK.

It's clear, therefore, that an automatic level can be very useful for the inexperienced hand. Some recording devices have built-in microphones, either stereo or mono. It may require you to switch settings on the machine to go between the built-in mic and the external mic, so make sure you read the instructions. Built-in mics can be handy if the student is using the equipment independently and would struggle with something else to think about. However, these mics can be catch-all solutions picking up absolutely everything and it is sometimes difficult to judge where you need to be in relation to the device. Make sure you keep the recorder as still as possible to avoid unwanted clicks and rattles. It really is a question of personal preference and need.

When you are more confident with recording you will no doubt discover that a hand-held external mic offers a better solution with greater flexibility. Just hold it still in the hand and make sure you keep any movements to a minimum. Many students want to hold a microphone like a rock or hip hop star, holding it almost against their mouths and at strange angle. Just place it in your hand and wrap your fingers around it. Before that, wrap the dangling microphone lead around your hand to keep the lead as short as possible. There is a good reason for this. Any dangling lead that brushes against you or a chair, table or anything else will appear loud and clear on the recording as 'mic-rattle'. It is an annoying clicking and clunking that the lead generates and which the mic picks up. You must also make sure that you keep your hand still on the mic. Moving the mic in your hand or tapping or rubbing it with your fingers will again cause it to rattle – it usually appears in the middle of word and is therefore impossible to edit out. It is also a good idea to point the microphone at a slight angle away from the person to be recorded rather than pointing directly at them. This can help with popping, whether the mic has a windshield or not (see page 64).

There is a simple way to understand this point. Clench your fist and then hold it against your mouth. Just say the word 'pop' and see what happens. You will feel a small pop of breath on your hand. When you are recording, that breath goes straight into the microphone. You will not notice that breath at the time you record, but you certainly will hear it out of the loudspeaker later. This may all sound rather detailed and unnecessary but it will make a difference between a reasonable recording and a great recording. Pops and clicks on a recording can ruin it, leaving you disappointed. Importantly, students will recognize it as inferior and not the high quality of sound they are used to hearing.

If you are working with young primary age children, it is probably best to hold the microphone yourself rather than let them do it. True, their young ears may not be quite so discerning and not so upset if it does not sound as clean as we would like, however, you may not enjoy the end result quite so much or possibly you might not be quite so keen to share the hard work as an example of best practice.

Additionally, microphones can be expensive and they tend not to bounce very well if dropped. A microphone is quite sensitive and it's a real hassle when they break because that is usually the end of the story.

There is one final point to note at this stage. As already suggested, the trick is to make sure you move your hand as little as possible when recording to eliminate noise. So to get a good and clear sound it will almost certainly be necessary to stand or sit rather closer than you would do normally to the person to be recorded. However, invading personal space is not a comfortable experience for many people.

Generally we do not allow many people voluntarily into our inner circle and those we do include the obvious examples such as family, partners, doctors, dentists, nurses and even hairdressers. You must now join that list, explaining that it only so you can keep that mic as still as possible.

However, it does not always work first time. I remember recording a businessman some years ago about his latest money-making venture. To get good illustrative sound we stepped out of his first floor office window onto the large flat roof beyond. With the recording underway I stood reasonably close to my interviewee asking questions as we went. Unfortunately he was less than comfortable with me invading his space so he periodically took a couple of steps back. It left me with no choice but to keep up casually as my microphone arm became somewhat outstretched only to be followed by another backward shuffle. As this impromptu dance continued for a while, the stark reality of the fact that we were on a first floor roof with no railings kicked in. This recording was clearly time limited or the consequences were fairly obvious. One of us was going to have to stop all this before the onset of multiple fractures and abrasions associated with two men falling from a roof.

Suffice to say, I wrapped it up in time but it does prove how tricky this can be for some people; they are just not comfortable.

So to recap, wrap mic leads around your hand, do not let any trailing lead knock against anything and keep your hand still on the mic. Move your hand as little as possible between interviewees or sound sources to keep the risk of mic rattle down to the minimum. Remember to watch those levels because sorting out distorted sound is impossible and adjusting quiet and loud voices are a chore, if not impossible, later.

There may be times when you want to record outside. Indeed it may be advantageous to record outside to illustrate the piece as discussed earlier in this chapter. The biggest nightmare to recording outside is wind noise. Even if your mic is fitted with a built-in metal windshield or a detachable foam shield, it will do little against the sound of a good breeze. It may look decidedly odd, but a good tip is to stand where you want to record and let the wind blow against your face. Turn around until it does and that way you will be able to tell which direction the wind is coming from and therefore if it will blow directly into your mic.

If the breeze is anything more than gentle then it would be a good idea to seek shelter of some sort, even against a fence or wall. On one recent occasion I had to assess a student recording someone outside in what turned out to be a fairly windy environment. I let the student make all the introductions and set the recording up. I stood, as suggested, in this breezy place moving around at right angles working out the direction of the wind. It looks odd I know, but it is usually a foolproof plan. My student did none of this, preferring not to look quite so stupid in a public place. The recording went well and back we went to school, to listen to the piece. It was unusable. All we could hear were a couple of voices struggling against the breeze that had transformed into gale force conditions by the time it came out of the loudspeaker.

I pointed out to the student my earlier right-angled performance to assess wind direction. He replied that he thought at the time that I was looking for somewhere to sit. Armed with this information, once again he went back to it after lunch on his own to a different location to turn around his previous disaster. And he did exactly the same again. It just goes to show you can lead a horse to water . . .

If your school or college has a studio, makeshift or otherwise, then there are a few more tips to take on board. Beware of the dreaded reverb again if your studio is in fact a converted classroom.

Again, you will hear it on the final recording if you are surrounded by clean, hard walls. If acoustic treatment such as baffle boxes are not a cost option at this stage, then look in cupboards, jumble sales or ask a neighbour for any old curtains. Big, heavy curtains draped on the hard walls will make a huge difference. Attach them to a pole if possible and hang that on hooks; then you can take the curtains down at the end if that is what you want. Keep the curtains fairly bunched up so the sound can get caught in the folds and you will have a low-cost or possibly no-cost solution to the problem. I have also spoken to voice-over artists who have carpeted walls in home studios or put PC towers in carpet-lined boxes to reduce the hum generated by computer fans. As ever there's no right answer, trial and error based on your budget is the best policy. With that sorted out we can concentrate on the recording.

Your studio will no doubt have a mic stand of some sort, either a boom or a lazy arm, so mic rattle no longer applies. That leaves you free to concentrate on the sound. You will find a separate section on different types of microphones in this book, but, put simply, different microphones do different things. You may want to bunch students around a microphone to record more than one person at a time. That may or may not be effective depending on the mics you have. If it is just one person recording at a time, then listening to the recording with headphones is a real advantage.

In professional radio, voice-over or music work, headphones are an absolute requirement. You cannot know how you sound if you do not use headphones in a studio where sound quality is taken for granted. Headphones will tell you immediately if you sound off-mic and distant, or if you are popping and distorted. They will also tell you if anything else you choose to play, like music, is louder or quieter than your voice. If you do not use headphones, you are flying blind. Also, do not adjust the volume once you have started the recording or the whole point becomes meaningless. The same applies to the mic levels.

For the sake of example we will assume your studio has a control desk such as *Alice* or *Soundcraft*. When you slide or push 'open' the fader on your desk, the needles in front of you will flicker across from zero toward six. Just watch those needles as you or anyone else speaks and set the mic levels so that the needles bounce around five and six. Open that fader to the top and leave it. If you need to adjust the volume, quieter or louder, then usually there is a separate volume knob above that fader to fine adjust the volume. That is where you should make adjustments, not with the fader. Then, every time you open the fader the volume setting will be right. If you move the fader up and down to different positions each time you use it, the levels will be all over the place and the recording a mess. It is a good idea to angle that mic on its stand slightly away from you as described earlier with the portable equipment. As before, this is to help with popping.

Now you can concentrate on where to sit in relation to the mic: how far it should be from your mouth or from the student? Is their voice naturally quiet and can we take advantage of that with close mic work? Do not force a voice into doing something it cannot do or it will no longer sound natural. If they are shouters, sit further back, watch those levels and click record. Somewhere is the sweet spot for their voice, some point in front of the mic where the voice sounds best, and here is a reason for headphones. Again this sounds rather grand and self-important and certainly not all these points are relevant for the one-off never to be repeated exercise. However, if a group is making a resource to be used by others, heard by a wider audience, then you will want to work to the highest standards as followed by professionals.

It really is not difficult, it is just a matter of practice and that is all. Regular users should find this all becomes second nature. It took me many years to work this out for myself because there was very little help in radio when I started. There was a widespread assumption that everyone knew what to do so nothing was ever explained. My early recordings in a studio are toe-curlingly bad because I had not bothered to work with the mic and treat it as a resource and a friend: one very small point to bear in mind about studios and microphones. I can't tell you how many times students and teachers have come to me saying that the equipment broke down just as they were about to record. I go through the process with them, they press record on the computer software, play some audio, perhaps a CD and look forlornly at the desk again as the sound cuts when they open, or push up the mic fader on the control desk. All they can hear is silence, which is proof enough that something has gone terribly wrong at the vital moment; except it has not, of course, if the desk was wired up properly by the engineer that installed it.

The sound is supposed to cut at that point to prevent an unpleasant blast of feedback, or 'howl round' as it is sometimes called – the sound from the mic would go out of those speakers and back into the mic, back out of the speakers and into the mic and so on at considerable speed. The result is that ear-shattering squeal caused when guest speakers wander absent-mindedly in front of the PA.

Two final pieces of advice. When you have finished recording make sure you save it on a computer or a disk if that is what you are using and make sure you know where you have put it. Students can be somewhat vague a week later when it comes to opening the file again.

I have saved the number one top tip for last. Whether you are using a portable device or the studio, the same advice applies. Make sure you switch the mic on and press record. I still have thoroughly unpleasant memories that I have managed to quash until now of the times I failed to follow that most basic function and got to the end of the recording only to find that I did not. I certainly was not the only young BBC reporter to record a challenging in-depth interview on a reel-to-reel *Uher* tape recorder only to find that I had not put a tape in. Looking at the empty spools with the interviewee is not something to be repeated in a hurry, trust me.

## Recording Dos and Don'ts

- Before you even start, make sure you know what it is you want to achieve.
- Stick to the spoken word whenever writing a script. Write can't, shan't, won't and don't because that's how we speak. Write in short sentences because that is how we tend to speak.
- Keep microphones and mic leads still when recording to avoid mic rattle noises. The rattle is difficult if not impossible to edit out and it will spoil your work.

- When recording outside in particular, listen to the sound around you and bear that in mind when editing the speech later.
- Do not record in echoey, reverberating rooms unless you want to use that to illustrate a point. Stand in a corner if there is no choice to minimize the reverberations. If reverberation happens in a makeshift school radio studio, buy heavy curtains or drape old blankets on the hard walls to soften the sound. Egg boxes on a wall are good cheap standbys if somewhat unattractive.
- Do not hold microphones too close to your mouth. If in doubt, outstretch your thumb and little finger on one hand and keep the mic that distance from your mouth.

Finally, the good edit is the one you cannot hear.

There is more detailed advice in chapters 3 and 7.

# 3 How to edit and mix audio

This chapter covers editing and mixing audio, moving from step-by-step basic top-and-tail editing to more sophisticated audio-package mixing for professional sounding classroom resources. It explains digital audio editing on computers and looks at the software options open to schools, teachers or students. Some of the jargon that can unnecessarily mystify and confuse is explained.

The main points featured in this chapter are:

- Basic audio editing techniques on a PC – if you can copy and paste a *Word* document, you can edit audio on screen
- Software options from paid for audio editing software such as *Adobe Audition* and free, open source editing software, such as *Audacity*
- Basic audio mixing on a PC
- Using background wildtrack audio
- Mixing music, sound effects or other voices in your production
- Saving as file-based audio to burn to CD or sending as an email
- The importance of imagination and creativity to a great mix
- Demystifying audio jargon.

## A background – flange, flutter and other novelties

If you can copy, paste and delete on a Word document, you can edit audio. The skills are essentially the same. Digital editing at its most basic is ridiculously simple these days so let's not be put off from the start. Students can do this, I can assure you. There is one very simple rule about editing. A good edit is an edit you cannot hear. If you hear a jump then it has not worked.

The clever bit is the sophisticated editing and mixing that comes with practice, as with all things in life. Purists will be shaking their heads in disbelief at such treason because mixing random words and sounds into a memorable experience is a craft, of that there is no doubt. And yes, that can still take years to fully master. But the average teacher and student will be happy, at least for now, to cut out the dodgy bits and top and tail the audio – in other words, edit up to the beginning and get rid of the tail end after the final words.

Thank heavens we have moved on from the days of editing on ¼-inch tape. Please do not even consider tape ever again, let it rest in peace. Peter Knowles spells out clearly that audio must now be recorded and edited digitally (see Chapter 7). This enables sound to be sent in various forms such as email and by mobile phone or burnt to CD. Tapes lasted for around 15 minutes or so if you wanted a good sound, but they had a nasty habit of getting wound around spools inside the machine. It would not be obvious until the recording was finished. Tape spools used to rewind at a zillion miles an hour, which is perfect for self-garrotting when your tie fell into the spools.

Digital editing is not only straightforward, it is also cheap and highly portable. You can edit on your computer – PC or Mac – or your laptop at school or at home. You can delete what you have done and start again with the same resource. Tape was not only expensive to buy but it was also awkward to wipe it clean of the previous audio.

Here is the best part though; the digital process is achievable by even young children and to my knowledge, no one has ever been strangled.

## Digital editing options

There are numerous digital editing packages available depending on whether you use PC or Mac. The music industry has its own favourites and the radio industry prefers others. *Garageband* is often mentioned by Mac users as a preferred package or even *ProTools*. There are different versions of *ProTools*, ranging from an individual computer to a recording studio set-up. It is not cheap to buy individual licences but the package is a powerful tool armed with an array of features. It tends to be a music technology package though and not favoured hugely by those that simply want to record speech-based features.

PC users tend to favour *Adobe Audition* which was formerly *CoolEdit*. At the time of writing there was no Mac version but rumours of changes have been persistent. *Adobe Audition* is a simple piece of editing software that even the most basic computer can handle. You will find yourself with a powerful multi-track recording studio on your computer, capable of everything you want to achieve and some things you had not thought of. You will probably have no other reason to look elsewhere at that point. *Sadie* is another system that appears in some professional radio studios but it is probably not for us at this stage – it rather falls into the 'sledgehammer to crack a nut' category.

It can be expensive for a single licence but always ask dealers for education licence prices because if you are buying it will be worth buying in bulk. It is not easy to recommend a specific piece of software for various reasons. Firstly, new versions are released all the time with new features. Some are specific and will be right for certain situations and skills levels and not others. There are packages that run on PC but not Mac and vice versa. There are so many out there that the best plan is to research what is available at the time and ask for advice from reputable dealers or other schools and colleges locally that may have already invested. Free trial versions are usually available to download from the various manufacturers' websites, so you do have the chance to try before you buy. There are also free-to-download open source editing packages.

*Audacity* is perhaps the best known free software and works with *Windows, Mac OS X, GNU/Linux*, and other operating systems. You can find it by simply typing *Audacity* into your preferred search engine. From there, the link to downloading can be confusing initially as you work out the mirror processes of downloading, but more experienced internet hands say they have no problems. From that point you are now in possession of a digital editing programme.

## The basics of digital editing

If you have never seen a digital edit package before, it can look daunting with buttons, icons, waveforms, colours and options all over the screen. Like all new experiences though, it looks more complicated than it actually is and you will not need all the functions initially, so do not be put off from the start.

Firstly, if you used a portable recorder of some sort, we need to get the audio to the computer. Most of the current generation of hard disk recorders use either a USB connection straight into the computer or a card reader.

Some audio needs to be transferred across in real-time; in other words played from the recorder and recorded in the computer as you go. So a three-minute recording will take three minutes to record in the computer. Sometimes you can drag and drop from the file created on your computer to the edit software.

- Open a new file on the audio editing software you have installed (for instance, *Adobe Audition* or *Audacity*). Once you have followed the instructions for that particular recording device, the audio should appear as a waveform on the screen, a series of waves going up and down.
- If the recording or transfer of the audio is too loud, then the waves will be very large, even a constant bank of colour if it has all gone wrong. You will need to go back to your recording setting in your computer. Click on the speaker icon on the bottom task bar of your computer until a large grey box appears with various sliders. It will appear as the Volume or Playback setting as default. What we need for now is the Recording setting.

- Click on Options, then Properties and another grey box appears. You should now have the option of selecting Recording.
- A new set of sliders will appear with varying names such as Line In, Microphone, What you Hear – it will depend on the sound card in your machine. If the computer is recording but the setting is too loud or too quiet, then simply adjust the selected fader up or down. It may be that all is silent and nothing is being recorded at all, in which case you should try selecting other faders to see which one works. Again, this depends on the sound card installed on your machine.

So now we have a waveform on our screen and this obviously is the raw audio with all its clicks, pops, umms and errs. You will also, no doubt, have some lead in sounds recorded before you settled into it all. So if you do nothing else you will at least want to tidy that up. This is very easy to sort out.

- Click on to your audio at the very start where you are settling down, knocking the microphone and clearing your throat.
- Hold down the mouse and highlight the waveform until you have reached the point where you start to make sense. With that audio now highlighted, press Delete on your computer keyboard. It's gone, never to be seen again, unless of course you were a little overzealous with you original highlighting and accidentally cut the crucial first couple of sentences that you actually do need, in which case, don't panic because there will be an Undo facility under Edit at the top of your screen. Here lies the beauty of it all. The Undo facility is a marvel and your less than perfect edit can be rescued as though nothing ever happened. You must, however, make sure that Undo is selected or face disappointment.

That then is editing at its most basic – highlight and delete.

To move on a little, what about making sure that the edit is absolutely clean and sharp and sits right next to the sound you want taken away or, more importantly, the sound you want to start with? Editing packages will have a Zoom facility somewhere within easy reach. It will be obvious. *Audition* has magnifying icons toward the bottom of the screen with a + symbol in one to zoom in and a − symbol in the other to zoom out. *Audacity* features a magnifying glass in the top left-hand corner. Click on that and the waves get larger as you zoom in, so obviously the more you click, the closer you get and the waves start to separate and splay out.

This now means you will be able to see quite clearly not just waves with peaks and troughs but the shape of individual words and sounds. This principle applies across the different digital editing packages. As it is impossible to describe them all in detail I will just concentrate for now on the free-to-download *Audacity*. Remember that the basics apply just about everywhere with similar facilities but with a different screen layout.

I ran an individual training session for someone recently who had used *Audacity* for some time, carefully editing away, who had no idea a zoom facility was there. He had not tried any of the available buttons. It's worth having a go at just clicking around to see what happens with a piece of audio you do not really need. No wonder this individual found editing something of a trial.

There will be a new problem to solve now. The very fact that you have zoomed into the audio means that it is quite likely that you have lost your place on the timeline and have no idea where the start is – it's over there to the left somewhere. Here's another button my partially frustrated student had not realized existed, that left him terribly grateful when identified. At the top left-hand corner, there are the six icons or buttons on *Audacity* where the magnifying glass is found. One of the six looks like two arrows joined together.

- If you hold your mouse over it for long enough it will tell you it is the Time Shift tool.
- Click that button and you can now go back to your waveform on the screen.
- Hold down the mouse button and by moving the mouse left to right you can move the audio left to right, so you can move the audio across until you find the start of the audio again. This, remember will be common across a variety of editing software packages but simply found elsewhere.
- The Time Shift is really useful in another example. If you record a second sound into *Audacity*, it will create a separate sound wave timeline under the first. Once completed, press the Time Shift tool again and you can move the second audio tight up to the end of the first or indeed fade it underneath the first. So the Time Shift operation makes placing any additional audio in exactly the right place extremely easy.

Other packages such as *Adobe Audition* allow you not only to move the sound along the timeline but over different timelines which is handy if your screen gets a little full and cramped. So we can now complete a simple edit and we can move audio around the screen along a timeline.

Back to the Zoom tool for a moment. Now we have mastered that, it is worth emphasizing once again its advantages. Getting close to the waveforms really helps to get a complete and precise edit. As stated earlier, you can not only hear but see exactly where and how a sound starts. You can see in detail every little click and annoying intrusion. A click will appear as a line initially, but go into the sound and you will see a large, sudden peak. Once you have zoomed in, it is easy to highlight and delete. The difficulty arises when the click, knock or pop is right at the beginning of a word, or even worse within a word. Just keep on zooming and with a little practice it is possible to take out almost that entire click that is spoiling the start of that word.

If the click is within the word then that is more of a dilemma. It may be best to leave alone and let it be. However, with confidence you may be able to see that sudden peak and remove a tiny slice without affecting the sound and clarity of the word. If not, just undo and accept there is nothing to be done about it.

One point about editing with strong background sounds, for instance, a commentary at a sports event, such as swimming or basketball, recorded by students. If your commentators slip up and make mistakes you will of course want to edit those mistakes out. It is quite possible you will still get away with it because the sounds, although loud, will be fairly constant. Water splashing in a pool surrounded by shouting and cheering onlookers will generally not fade in or out, so you should be able to edit out small mistakes and notice any jumps at the edit points. That level of constant background illustration is generally not a problem.

Problems occur when the background sound changes. For example, students are recording a 'drive safely' public information trailer for English coursework. You have your students recording on the pavement outside school or college to get those traffic sounds to illustrate the pieces. Back in the classroom, listening to the tracks and you notice a couple of edits. It's likely that the background sound comes and goes as the traffic moves around.

This is one example where you do have to listen carefully to what is happening. Usually we would hear the vehicles approaching, then passing and not pay any attention to it because that is what we expect. However, if the edit needs to happen as the vehicle approaches, you will notice because the car or truck will appear to sound as though it has stopped somewhat abruptly and then restarted sometime later or not at all. It may not seem a big problem right now but if that happens on your recording you will realize how strange that sounds.

If you want to change the sequence of your audio, for instance, move one short sound or just a few words to a different place on the timeline, then all you need do is copy and paste.

- Highlight the audio you want to move, click Copy and move the cursor to where the sound needs to go.
- Now click Paste, remembering to delete the audio from where you brought it, otherwise you have it twice. It is exactly the same as copy and paste in a Word document – it is that easy.
- Then all you have to do is edit the gaps. If you need to put some extra silence in there because the sounds or words are too close together, then select the Silence option on the task bar. Most, if not all packages will allow you to do that and determine how long you want that silence to be – one second, ten seconds, however long you wish.

There is one other trick here worth mentioning if you want to add that little extra space between words; maybe silence is not practical because you have recorded students against a constant background sound.

- Listen to a point where they have stopped speaking and that constant sound is precisely that. Then copy that small piece of background sound and paste it into the point where you need that extra space. Paste it a few times if that is what is required, edit and tidy up and that is another problem solved. You will soon get into the habit of listening closely and being aware of what is happening around you and that saves a great deal of time when editing later. The same obviously applies to music playing in the background – music as part of a mix is outlined in the next section.

Editing at the level just illustrated is simple but effective. The skill that moves the process on is to mix those sounds and edit to the point where the listener has no idea anything has been done. So another simple piece of advice about editing speech is to edit against a breath. It is easy when in something of a rush to edit two breaths together, particularly if that person recorded several takes. The end result is distinctly odd and makes the recorded individual sound as though they are in the middle of an asthma attack. They won't thank you for it.

# Mixing audio

Don't turn over the page because, again, this is easier than you might think. Even a simple mix can turn your audio into a professional sounding product. Like editing, mixing can be as complex or as simple as you like. It may be that you would like to mix a couple of voices together such as a narrator or voice-over and a guest or interviewee.Or perhaps you want to record background sounds into your piece. That can, of course, remove the problem of editing with strong background sounds. Record the sounds first and put that in later over the top of edited voices. You will sometimes see background sounds or effects referred to as wildtrack or FX.

Maybe you have multiple voices or sounds and want to create a short jingle. Just be aware that if you want to include commercially available music as part of your mix that will be heard by the public, you may have copyright issues that need checking and will need to consider royalty-free music. Obviously if the music is recorded by students themselves then there is no problem. As before, it is impossible to go through every piece of edit software and explain what happens but again the same principles apply – it may just mean you need to look around the screen.

As mentioned in the previous section on editing, there will be a Time Shift button to select which means you can move audio along a timeline or maybe across timelines. However, some edit packages, such as *Adobe Audition,* require you to switch from a single waveform screen to a multiple edit and mix screen, but on the open source *Audacity* everything takes place on the one screen in front of you, there is no choice.

For the sake of examples we will look at *Audacity*. When you record or download a second piece of audio it will automatically create a second timeline directly under the first. One point to note: *Audacity* works within its own system and will not allow you to dump WMA (Windows Media Audio) files onto your screen as an import. You will need to convert them first.

- Edit the various timelines so you are ready to go. Look at your software to see if there is a Mute button at the side of the timeline. It may be titled Mute or simply given the letter M. Mute will allow you to silence that track or tracks while you listen to just one. There may also be a Solo button which will silence all others tracks at one click enabling you to concentrate on just one.
- The next function you will likely want to select is fading audio either in or out. Under the Effects option at the top task bar on many packages you will see a drop down panel. On *Audacity* you will see a Fade In and Fade Out option and this will allow you to do exactly what it suggests. Highlight the beginning or end of your audio, select the appropriate option from the effects drop down panel and click. The audio will have gone from nothing if the Fade In option was selected and will have gradually climbed to the normal volume.

On the screen you will see the waves again go from nothing, gradually increasing in size. Fading in then allows you to bring in a secondary sound, such as a sound effect, background sound or music underneath the first voice. There may be times when a sudden start is entirely appropriate but a fade is a useful option. That is fine as it stands but the control you have over what happens is a little limited. Edit packages will allow you to decide when and where that fade takes place. Again each package will have its own method but it should be obvious by looking in Tools or Effects options on the task bars.

*Audacity* has a curious looking button which is in that group of six buttons. It is another facility that came as a surprise to the student previously mentioned who had been using the software for sometime.

- Click on the button that has two white triangles with a blue line in-between.
- Click back onto the audio again and you will see tiny white dots appear along the top of the audio.
- Click further along and you will create more dots and so on.
- Then click on one of those dots, holding down the mouse button and drag the dots down. You will see the waves moving to the centre which is in fact, reducing the volume, creating a fade mid-way or at any point you choose.

Whichever software package you have bought, the point is you can now fade the sound right down along the entire track if necessary, increasing it at certain points and dropping it right down again. So if the music plays underneath voices, an illustrative background sound is there underneath several voices if necessary. It will make a big difference to the finished sound, and as you have now discovered, it is very easy to achieve. Adjusting the volume levels is a matter for your ears – no one can tell you what level the volume should be set.

Listen through a pair of headphones or decent speakers. The speakers in laptops and many desk computers can be poor quality and not really adequate for monitoring sound levels at this stage of our project. Even a cheap pair of headphones allowing you to really concentrate is better than a quiet and metallic laptop speaker. Speakers, or monitors as they are often called in professional studios, are usually of the highest quality with fairly steep price tags to go with them. Listening is key to all edit and mixing.

You can watch levels on your recording device, sound desk or computer, you can look at what you have got on the screen, but it is your ears that should make the final decision. If it sounds right it is right. Walk away and do something else for a while if needed, then come back and listen again but be honest with yourself – if it does not seem quite perfect at this stage then go back and make some very minor adjustments to the levels of your tracks.

So now we can make simple edits, we can introduce second or further tracks and we can fade them and mix them together. If you are happy with the mix you have created with several timelines now on your screen, then it may be possible to mix everything together as one track. If that is an option on your software then it is a good idea to take advantage. It tidies everything up and reduces the chance of ruining your hard work by accidentally moving a track slightly out of synch. Of course it does mean that once you have opted to do that, you are committed and you cannot change your mind.

## Effects and another language

*Change pitch, change speed, normalize, wah-wah, reverb, click removal, amplify, pan, echo chamber* and my own favourite, *phaser*.

As mentioned at the start of this chapter, working with audio will introduce you to a new language of words that appear to be English but make little or no sense. *Phaser* has nothing to do with Captain Kirk on the Starship Enterprise. It is of course a sound effect and not easy to describe in mere words. However, if you are or were a fan of 1960s and 70s progressive rock music you will be familiar with phasing. It is that curious slow *wah wah* style of effect that seems to roll in and out of the sound, bending the music and voices slightly as it goes.

This is hardly a first choice effect that you would select for a basic speech piece, but you could use this as part of your armoury when making a jingle, for example. The same applies to any of these effects. Used sparingly and appropriately, they can help produce really quite dramatic audio snippets.

Look around your digital edit software because these effects will be there somewhere. Sometimes they have different titles and not all packages will have all effects; some can be downloaded later as additional add-ons. *Echo chamber* does what it says and most software will allow you to choose the degree of echo. It is easy to go seriously overboard here to the point where you can no longer make sense of what you did originally. Add echo and listen carefully; again, a number of packages will allow you to preview what you are trying before committing yourself to that new sound. Even if you change your mind at that point, there is always the Undo feature. *Normalize* and *amplify* are essentially the same feature in that they will allow you to increase or decrease the volume of what you have recorded, so you could take a track up three decibels, six decibels and so on. Some have preset fade options so you choose a fade that goes up sharply or slowly. I have even seen one called squiggly that allows the sound to go up, down, up and down randomly, changing the speed at the same time. What you would use it for I cannot imagine. *Pan* is useful if you really want to make a point in stereo. *Pan* allows you to move the sound from left to right speaker or vice versa.

So you can make a sound move across the stereo field, or it can be very effective if you have just two voices. Put one voice to the left and the other to the right which is a simple way of adding extra interest to an otherwise straightforward recording. I will not attempt to explain all these features because some, I guarantee, you will never use.

However, here is another useful trick: click Eliminator or Noise Reduction to rescue audio awash with background hissing and other troublesome noises. This does take some practice though so it is best to leave this alone for now, but bear it in mind that the option is there when you are ready. This is important. Keep it simple and manageable for now so neither teacher or student is disappointed.

## Save the audio

It is rather obvious of course but the audio needs to be saved. You do have several options as a rule and you must make sure you know what format you have saved your audio in. Some edit software packages allow to save audio in variety of means; WMA, WAV (waveform audio format) and MP3 are the most familiar and you are most likely to use.

For good quality sound it is hard to beat WAV files. However, the files can be huge when stored so a regular clear out of drives may be required as they will get full. If you want to send your audio elsewhere, to other students or teachers at a different school by email, then it would be wise to avoid large WAV files because your connection is more likely to drop out before you have finished sending – that is if your server can cope in the first place.

Generally MP3s are favoured as podcast audio and for sending as an email but they can lose a little in sound quality, again when compared to WAV. That would only be noticeable in most cases with a good set of speakers or headphones so it is not really an issue. It is not always the saving of audio that is an issue but opening it up afterwards. I have seen student after student struggle to open audio that appears to be on the screen but ends up corrupted. Often it is because the student has saved the audio in one unusual format and then tries to open it up in another. It is all too easy to lose audio or to find it and then be unable to do anything with it. It is probably best to supervise audio being saved as a WAV and then the problem should be solved. The open source *Audacity* uses its own format to save in. If you should need to open that saved audio in a different programme, such as *Adobe Audition*, mentioned earlier, or other similar programmes, then you will need to use the Export as WAV function which converts the audio into a WAV file. If you open a music CD on your computer and want to put that music into *Audition* or other edit software, then you will be able to drag the WMA file that appears on the screen when you place the CD in the CD drive. Hold the mouse down, drag the WMA file onto a timeline and it will appear in seconds as waves on the screen that can in turn be saved as a WAV file.

That makes the mixing so much easier. Sending audio via email is a real advantage and can create new options. Projects that start in one school or even one country can then be sent to another for completion, and then back again to be listened to and commented on. If your server at school is not keen on these huge files as an email, then search the internet for programmes that allow that kind of traffic. I have used free services such as *You Send It* to move audio between schools as MP3s to great effect.

## A round up

Editing and mixing can be a rewarding experience and I have yet to meet a student that is not impressed by the end result.

To reiterate a point flowing through this book. Even a few minutes spent carefully editing and mixing will produce professional sounding results again and again; it just isn't that easy with video. Students are a discerning audience so they know instinctively when it is right. Audio products from downloads to podcasts to digital radio and traditional analogue radio have never been more popular in the UK. At the time of writing, 91 per cent of the UK population – 45.6 million people – now tune into radio.

Students I have worked with on projects using the methods detailed in this chapter realize very early that they produce materials to a standard they and their peers recognize. Computer digital-edit programmes with all the multi-functions they provide do allow creativity to run wild and create sounds that would have been impossible for school and college students a few short years ago. It matters not whether these students are 11 or 18, further and higher education or even primary school children. They can all try their hand and will be surprised at what they can achieve because they will tell you so, and you can see the surprise and growing confidence on their faces. We have only considered the basic outline in this chapter but nevertheless we can now record, complete simple audio edits and mixes.

Once these skills have been tried a few times, it will become apparent that creativity can move closer to the top of the agenda. From here on, the chances of teacher becoming mentor, even co-producer with students becomes a reality. The technology allows creativity with an end product to take place that was not possible a generation before. With that out of the way, and a means now available, students and mentors can get down to the serious business of having fun, sharing skills, developing media literacy, personal awareness, self confidence, cooperation and collaboration, personalizing learning and a route towards burgeoning social enterprise.

Technology of this sort has opened up an enormous number of ways that young people can express themselves. The technology of the workplace and the classroom are now one and the same which again has positive benefits for those considering the 14–19 diplomas in Creative and Media. Now it is perfectly possible to spend £100 on editing and mixing in school; 20 years ago it would have cost the industry £200,000.

With digital edit software on my computer at home, I feel it is time to admit that much of my radio news packages in the couple of years before I left the BBC were actually not edited in plush studios at all. They were produced, along with a couple of series and a documentary or two, in my dining room at home.

I feel better now I have got that off my chest.

# The interview: how
# 4 to construct interviews
# to extend learning

Interviews can make superb classroom resources for a variety of curriculum subjects and situations ranging from citizenship to history and mock job interviews. The interview captures the moment, the impression and the emotion.

In this chapter, interview techniques are explained in detail including the use of the microphone, when to use open and closed questions, and how body language can help in producing memorable audio. There are also examples of what can go wrong and how to make sure it does not happen to you.

The main points featured in this chapter are:

- How to use recorded interviews across the curriculum and how to use recorded interviews to prepare for job or college interviews
- How to use recorded interviews as a bridge to the community and extend learning
- How to construct an interview
- Open questions and closed questions
- The importance of the five Ws: Who, What, Where, When, Why and How
- The importance of smiling on the radio and the 'noddy'
- Basic interview recording techniques
- Why writing questions in advance can be a bad idea.

## The value of the interview

The interview is a tricky one for many students. As with all things, some just get it with little or no encouragement, others really struggle with the idea.

So when would the interview come into play? Citizenship or PSHE is an obvious starter. We could get the local mayor in to talk about the work of the council and all things democratic. Worthy perhaps and a tad dull for the average teenager. But there are plenty of other useful people out there who would welcome the chance to get into schools and whom the students really ought to know about. The community is awash with fascinating stories and real life experiences; some of those stories are, of course, slipping through our fingers, disappearing over time.

A school can have a real place here in capturing those stories before they have gone. How many people are there with vivid and accurate memories of what actually happened during the Second World War in your town, city or village? And for how much longer? They will have inspiring stories of citizenship at its most heightened; not just hardship and danger but a real deep sense of community that sadly may seem improbable to some students today.

It does not always work of course. I lived for some years next to a wonderful man who for a time ran the airport on the Falkland Islands and was honoured by the British government for the part he played in the island community. His wife also took part in the Falklands radio station; a tight-knit way of life with so many genuinely fascinating stories that could be not just entertaining but frankly educational as well. The political views are not relevant here; it is the story that counts. I tried again and again to tease out some of the many tales he clearly had to tell retired and back in the east coast of England. While he was prepared to reveal tantalising morsels in private over the inevitable glass of whiskey that always miraculously appeared, he was never inclined to do so in front of a microphone. I badly wanted radio listeners, my community, to share the experience, but he was a shy and private man who is sadly no longer here. The stories have gone forever.

And that is the point; catch them while you can and let students relish a real learning experience from someone who is experiencing or has experienced a moment of life.

Childcare students talking to the single parent group. Is that a negative message or real life? Is there real guidance and genuine learning to be gained from talking to that young mum or dad and how they put parent theory into parent practice? Bear in mind, of course, that this is a shared experience, because although the students will clearly benefit from this interview, the interviewee will also gain something along the way.

When was the last time they could sit down and talk through their life, putting into order thoughts and ideas? They are also talking to, by and large, an interested audience – students who want to know. This is another clear example of schools as a bridge within the community – the concept of education as a shared experience, building values, schools and community engaging with each other, and appreciating that community's history and future to some extent.

And what if we were then to make all these interviews available to the wider community as a shared resource, an audio library in effect? That is a powerful record of who we are; not just a collection of undeniably valuable local reference documents, journals and papers held at the local library, but a talking library of our heritage.

I once arranged for some Year 8 students to interview a man who remembered seeing The Beatles live in concert. They sat somewhat bewildered at tales of screaming, inconsolable girls, sobbing over the inescapable fact that Paul McCartney was not likely to be rushing out to buy them an engagement ring after the show. The boys in the audience, the Year 8 interviewers were told, supported Ringo on the provocative grounds that the girls did not. And the single most baffling fact for the young students was that no one in the cinema, where The Beatles played, could hear anything anyway. They also heard how this man, then a teenager himself, got together a tea chest and pole and created something that resembled a stand up bass.

The interview was packaged with a couple of clips of Beatles tracks and clips from the internet. It became an utterly compelling basis for a history lesson on the 1960s to Year 9 students one summer term. That was complemented with more material from a Bubble car owner, from a local astronomer on the Apollo 11 moon landing with the obligatory Neil Armstrong quote from the internet, and from a fashion expert on the mini skirt and growth of teenage materialism. That becomes history that connects with today.

Local people, maybe known to some of the children, were talking about their hobbies, fascinations and personal experiences. The local BBC radio station already had a couple of 1960s archive clips on hand that they could share; the launch of the Telstar satellite that gave us a taste of international communication for the first time and a clip about a near riot between Mod and Rockers which became a questionable British seaside institution for a few years.

Of course compiling, recording, editing and building such resources into lessons takes time, and that is and will always be an issue, but once burnt to CD, it's done and can sit there for many future years. It can also be shared with other schools and colleagues to enable them to enjoy that best practice. The students and other department members can help and share the research and compilation. History moves from the page into real life.

## How to construct an interview

The interview can be tricky for many students to get right. The most obvious point often repeated is to make sure that you do not ask closed questions. Yes or No as an answer marks a pretty short conversation but it is, nevertheless, the most common mistake in my experience.

Closed questions such as 'This is a good idea isn't it?', 'You agree that we should do this?' confirm the statement you have just made. Closed questions are easy to answer clearly, they are quick to answer and they put control of the interview with the interviewer. However, it is far from fascinating as a listening experience. This may well be useful as an audio questionnaire technique and, of course, closed questions are often used in the classroom to check learning. Aren't they?

Open questions put the conversation squarely back with the interviewee. So a question that begins with 'Tell me about' or 'Can you explain how' forces a response. They ask people to reflect on something and consider a reply and invariably such questions give an opportunity for feelings and emotions, be they humour, anger or simply facts.

Words such as 'How' and 'Why' are often simple ways of getting facts to the front, and are not so wildly divorced from our normal day-to-day conversations, yet the process of the interview can still be uphill. To start with it is a forced conversation. The interview is not like a chat with a friend that often meanders around; the interview is a means of getting to the point, and the interviewer subtly controls a good interview. The interviewer should be absolutely clear about where the interview is going, yet keep an open mind to responses for which he or she could not possibly have planned for. If that is the case, go with it for a while and see where the interview takes you, but bear in mind that you will want to get back on track quickly.

I was a tutor and assessor for a group of postgraduate radio students for a while. On one observation visit, I sat through an interview that clearly fascinated the student greatly; it was a favoured subject of his. Unfortunately he was so enthusiastic that the conversation zig-zagged all over the place, picking up bits and pieces as he went. Naturally he was thrilled with the result after recording over 20 minutes but unfortunately he only needed three when edited down. The end result was just about incomprehensible because he had no structure to the conversation at all. In other words, he had no idea where he was going when he started.

So with that in mind we can probably see a way forward. The most effective interview is a combination of both open and closed questions and if there is any trick at all to this, it is knowing when to implement either. And that really is a matter of experience. The skilled practitioner will know when the time is right and know when to apply the pressure and then when to back away with a line of questioning. They will also know when to make a statement rather than ask a question – or both – 'So that's reached a conclusion and it's time to move on then. What's next?'

It may sound as though this is bordering on cliché, but smile when you are interviewing someone, and nod your head occasionally. There was a long-standing tradition in television interviews years ago to film the 'noddy shot' after the interview had finished. Basically television news used one film camera, as with one video camera today. With the interview done and the guest bid farewell, the camera could be turned around to the interviewer who remained there. Into thin air, the interviewer repeated a couple of questions asked of their guests and duly nodded at the end a couple of times. This, of course, gives a body language sign to the guest and viewer; in this case, that we are listening and interested in what they are saying. Having done that myself elsewhere in my career, I can confirm that talking intently to an empty space where someone stood a few minutes ago is about as strange as it gets, with a wide assumption that strong drink has taken hold.

Perhaps that is the reason why television has all but abandoned such practices. Obviously, there's no such option using audio, at least as far as the listener knows, but a nod here and there will be appreciated by your audio guest. A small smile will generate a relaxing response, and although an occasional nodding of your head may seem strange at the time to you, it will reassure your guest, I can promise you.

Do not, under any circumstances resort to the 'uh huh' or 'mmm' sound that we normally use when talking. It is immensely annoying when you play back the audio and just gets in the way.

If there should be a loud sudden noise, such as a door slamming, or your interviewee gets completely tongue-tied, then do not be afraid to ask the interviewee to repeat their answer. It is not being rude and will help the interviewee produce a better impression of what he or she has to say.

Wear headphones when you record if you must but personally I would not bother, they are a distraction, get in the way and I have yet to hear a real advantage in that. See Chapter 2 for more details on recording techniques.

## When could interviews be used?

Away from the obvious media exercise, how could this be relevant to other classroom situations?

I have used the interview technique with classes of 15- and 16-year-old Year 11 students leading up to work experience sessions. I have also worked with the same age group prior to Industry Days that are practised by some schools where industry partners go in to give mock job interviews. It's simply a twist on the technique. This time instead of the students thinking of the questions and conducting an interview, I interview them using open and closed questions in the way a job interview would be conducted. The process is recorded on a hard disk recorder and played back in private if that suits the student better. It has proved very successful, not simply as a mock job interview but because the student can hear exactly what they sound like.

They can hear whether they sound bored or monotone, and it's quite possible that this is the first time they have really heard how others receive them. It is a straightforward matter after that to get them to realize what impact they are having with an employer, or at the Sixth Form College or Further or Higher Education interview. They will, of course, say 'Do I really sound like that?' because everyone does. They will not appreciate that their own voice rattles and vibrates around in their heads before ending up in their own ears, and that can sound slightly different to the sound that departs from their mouths and ends up rattle-free in someone else's ears.

The next logical step of course is to get students to take your place and interview each other. This can have mixed success depending on the confidence of the students concerned. If nothing else it all helps toward improved speaking and listening skills and an awareness of the skill.

In English, we could catch a short interview with a local police officer that could be converted into public information speed-kills type trailers.

In performing arts, some of these collected conversations can be converted into short plays and improvised performances based on those recollections.

In music, an interview with a local independent record shop owner will no doubt reveal what it is really like on the local band and gig circuit, putting those music lessons back to a sense of reality; how that music practice can in fact lead to actually entertaining people with all the huge personal benefits that spring from that as a performer. This is not likely to take up a great deal of time during the lesson, but as a short lesson starter or as a plenary we can now relate that peripatetic guitar lesson to a real audience. We can also hear, perhaps, about what music actually sells. And like so much of modern life, it becomes a fashion statement for our audio library to be smiled at years or maybe months later as the next genre takes over.

Mid-teen students invariably run out of steam fairly early and after a couple of brief questions and equally brief answers the cry goes up 'I can't think what else to say'. In truth of course most adults are the same. We feel self-conscious, particularly if we are wheedling a microphone. It's a false situation. We do not normally talk to people in the way that an interview is conducted. Again, making that sound like a conversation and creating a relaxing atmosphere for the interviewee is a skill in its own right.

# Interview recording technique

The technique that worked for me time and again as a professional interviewer and in the classroom was to ignore the microphone first. If you are holding this bulbous black stick attached by a cable to a plastic box of some sort then it can't help but get in the way. People are instantly uneasy and the usual reaction is; 'I don't want to talk into that thing'. I have also had many occasions were otherwise super-confident people talk freely when the microphone is switched off but when switched on they become strangely fluent in gibberish with a fixed facial expression.

So after many attempts at trial and error, I now sit or stand with the interviewee whilst holding a recording device down by my side or even slightly behind my back, if possible, along with the mic. If sitting down, put the recorder away on the floor assuming that there is a separate mic and the lead is long enough. Again the mic can be down, out of the way and out of sight.

That gives time to start a warm-up pre-amble conversation with the guest about whatever it is you want to talk about. So clearly if the guest is an outside visitor it can be the usual conversation starters with strangers – talk about the weather, their journey here and so on, introducing the real topic bit by bit, asking real questions occasionally along the way. By doing that you can assess whether some of your questions will get anything like a sensible and valuable response. If they do, then make a mental note of their reply and make sure you ask that question at some point. If the question hits a wall, discard it. Time and again though, this technique brought other points to light that I could not have predicted in my planning. There may be other issues I did not know about, reactions I had not expected and other areas that could be explored.

So in a sense this is a practice interview but because I dripped these questions in over a casual conversation, I suspect many if not most of my interviewees did not really appreciate what I was up to – at least the first time around. Established guests who have done this before will get to know what you are up to and understand the process.

While this is taking place I always made sure my body language was as relaxed as possible along with my vocal tones. I would not want to give any impression at this point that this was an interview about to happen. Gradually my slouching would be less so and I would attempt to fix eye contact and maintain it. Now I can tell my interviewee that we are going to start recording, I can maintain that eye contact and slowly move the microphone up toward them around nine to ten inches or so from their mouths, hopefully without them realizing what has happened.

So to cater for that lead-in time, make sure you ask a dummy question, one that you are not really bothered about but sounds right. If they say something interesting then that is fine but if not, there's no harm done and at least they have the chance to settle down again.

This may sound somewhat over complicated and convoluted for what should be a simple enough exercise. How difficult can it be to interview someone; student, outside guest or otherwise? However, when you try interviewing for the first time, it is then that you realize how tricky this can be. Our aim is for this not to sound like a formal interview at all but a controlled conversation where the interviewer is in charge. We have heard interviews so many times ourselves and of course, it always sounds easy.

There are just a couple of outstanding points with regard to questions. Do we write questions down or do we ad-lib and do we let the interviewee know in advance what we are going to say?

There's nothing terribly wrong with writing questions down, but it does sound forced and emphasizes that awkwardness that is already present. In a normal classroom situation, it is perfectly acceptable. But if we were to interview a senior figure in our community for a citizenship topic, maybe even a fast food outlet for our Healthy Schools programmes, it would be best left undone. Practise a few questions in your head because you should know where this conversation is going.

Alternatively, write a few bulletin points down and try to follow the thread of the conversation. You want emotional responses rather than rehearsed and managed sound bites that the interviewee has had time to prepare. And never, ever, let them take the microphone from your hands. It is a guaranteed certainty that the microphone will end up too close to their mouths, will rattle constantly through the recording and then at the hand-changeover times. It's not a baton, and it is yours. Guard jealously.

To recap on a couple of points:

- Keep the microphone around nine inches or so from your mouth and the interviewee's, and move it as little as possible – otherwise you will pick up mic rattle and it will occur at a vital point where you cannot edit it out. It just happens that way to irritate us.
- Find a quiet room if it is just a conversation that you want or you want to include some music or sound effects later. Otherwise find a place with ambient sounds that help tell the story; it will be much more interesting. Record some of that background sound as wildtrack to use later if that is appropriate.
- Prepare some questions in your head but do not read them from a script because it will sound forced and artificial. Do not give your guest questions in advance so they can prepare bland, antiseptic answers.
- Do be prepared to interrupt, albeit politely, if you feel the need to move things on. Again this is not being rude; it is about you helping the guest sound better and about keeping your listening student audience with you.

# Part 2

---

# Incorporating audio
# into your lessons

# 5 Lesson ideas: how to use audio across the curriculum

With recording, editing, mixing and interviewing explained, this chapter (and Chapter 6) gives specific advice and ideas on how to use audio in the classroom across a range of curriculum areas from the sciences to mathematics, media, sport and geography and in a range of forms, such as audio blogs and books. There is information for primary school teachers and secondary school teachers and examples of after-school clubs and tips for special educational needs coordinators. The resources in this chapter outline tasks, outcomes and how to achieve them with hints on differentiation and personalization.

The main points featured in this chapter are:

- Ideas for media including BTEC and the 14–19 Creative and Media Diploma Line
- How to make a radio trail or commercial, including differentiation, peer evaluation and script writing using the AIDA formula
- Ideas for audio across the curriculum
- The benefits for special educational needs
- How to use audio in primary schools and after-school clubs with audio postcards and radio programmes
- How to record your own audio books to aid literacy
- How to use audio to create classroom resources with a long shelf life that can be easily adapted and altered
- Audio for *PowerPoint* or *MovieMaker*
- Audio as a public relations tool for websites, podcasts and emails.

## Suggestions for specific tasks across the curriculum

A good idea is a good idea. Therefore much of what is described in this chapter can be adapted one way or another for all kinds of subject areas and for all ages of children and students, from primary to secondary and college. Just experiment. A task may well fit a given media coursework project but it could easily be adapted to a vast range of subject areas and situations with a little imagination.

This is by no means an exhaustive list, just some ideas to get us started. Creativity and the willingness to take risks are what matters here. As ever, the answer is yes; what was the question?

This section starts by looking at secondary schools and then primary schools.

## Media
### 14–19 Diploma Lines

Secondary education in the UK is going through what is arguably its biggest shake up in a generation and will impact on every school and college in the country. The new Diploma Lines for 14 to 19 year olds will roll out until at least 2013. The first 14 lines of learning will cover subjects as diverse as Environmental and Land Based Studies, Society, Health and Development, Engineering, and Creative and Media. It is designed to be a lasting opportunity to marry the needs of industry and commerce with what education can provide. Traditionally the two have had an uneasy relationship.

At time of writing, the first five diplomas, including Creative and Media, were almost ready to roll out. In theory, any child should have access to any Diploma Line of their choice by 2013 when all the subject areas have been piloted, thoroughly tested and evaluated. It is expected that students taking the Diplomas will have a broad-based education, but focus on areas of principal learning – in other words the subject area they have chosen.

Clearly audio can have a significant place in the education toolkit of the teacher in this new world. As far as Creative and Media is concerned, it can take centre stage in a number of units. As the units were still in an official draft form at the time of writing, what follows is a suggestion based on what has been published.

So by way of example, one 60-hour Level 2 unit is entitled Campaign. The units are suitably open to allow approaches from differing creative viewpoints. The intention, it would seem, is to encourage students to use their creative skills in the way they see appropriate to solving a problem, which in this case, is how to get a message across to a target audience. It is fairly standard media fodder which, by and large, is concerned with producing products that someone will want to watch, read, buy, consume or take part in. Expressive arts students will look at this from a different view and may create theatre to get a point across.

Students will investigate existing campaigns and then work out a campaign and message they want to put across. Putting across that campaign, as suggested in draft modules, could involve leaflets and print adverts, a piece of theatre or a series of radio commercials. So to achieve the learning outcomes, students will not only have to plan a campaign and assess how it will be evaluated, but also have to produce the materials.

This unit is ideally suited to audio work because legal and ethical considerations will also play a key part. Radio advertising is subject to strict rules and regulations about claims that can be made but podcasts are still unregulated.

Topics such as this have featured in media qualifications in the past and achieving the learning outcome on distribution has always been problematic and invariably on a small-scale. However, this unit does point towards web-based distribution and even RSL (restricted service licence) radio stations as possible solutions to the problem. It might be wise to double-check the *Ofcom* regulations if using an RSL in the UK to make sure no agreements are being breached by the subject matter of the campaign – for example, religion is a no-go area.

There is an acknowledgement that assessing the effectiveness of a campaign using these broadcast technologies is tricky compared with a localized and small-scale campaign. There will need to be evidence of review, planning and assessment as the unit progresses. Again students do not have to choose automatically to write that planning, but they can think of using video or audio diaries or web blogs to note down progress.

Audio diaries are incredibly easy to do; they just require organization, careful logging and storage – useful skills in their own right. To précis this, at the end of a given time, students can simply record what they have done, how they did it and perhaps what they did not do. They can record into a PC or laptop with a cheap microphone, straight into free software such as *Audacity*. A quick top and tail, tidy up and save. It is that simple and takes minutes. They could also record a brief part of a conversation at a production meeting, with a focus group, or with a teacher explaining what they have done – real, on the spot evidence of what took place, and it takes next to no time.

All this could apply to numerous units and to numerous Diploma Line subject areas. Audio need not always be the vehicle or subject matter but it is also a valid and effective means of self and peer assessment.

## BTEC

I have used this first project, outlined below, on radio trails and commercials for BTEC Media courses but this could also be appropriate for English and literacy sessions and other media classes of differing age groups.

It must be stressed that although I have used these ideas successfully with BTEC Media students in the past, none of these lessons is officially approved by any exam board. I include these merely as suggestions of easily manageable projects that do not necessarily need huge resources. The principles behind them could just as easily be altered and developed for other subject areas such as English and modern foreign languages.

This task focuses on speaking and listening but also on creative writing. This can be a simple small team or individual project depending on group size, resources and time. Although straightforward, the students are developing some highly sophisticated communication skills. This is not just about writing in the spoken word, but communicating to an audience in the way they expect to be spoken to.

## Task: To make a radio trail

**Outcomes: the ability to write in the spoken word and the ability to motivate an audience**

If time is limited to one lesson, then get the students to concentrate on writing a trail script bearing in mind that the script must be in the spoken word not written word.

If further time is available, get the group or student to record their trail on a hard disk recorder or similar device, download and edit on *Audacity*, *Audition* or similar edit software. Provide students with suitable music to meet the theme of the trail if that is appropriate or ask students to supply their own and get them to source sound effects from the internet. They should then record the music and effects to the software, edit and mix.

**Extension exercise**

Ask students to use the same principles to write and produce a radio commercial for a product of their choice – for example, an unusual flavour for an instant noodle snack in a pot such as fish and chip flavour, beef and strawberry – anything that will get their imagination going. This has always worked well in the past because it opens the doors to the use of sound effects and humour. They must bear in mind the target audience of the pot snack, and the fact that a young audience will tolerate humour that an older audience would consider silly.

**Differentiation**

Each student can approach this task at his or her own level. They must all understand that they cannot get the task wrong: they can make a bad judgement but they cannot get it wrong. A trail or a commercial is only a bad idea if it fails to motivate people but the only way of knowing is to try it for real.

Encourage students to take risks with ideas and be as creative as possible. If an idea does not work out, it does not matter. No professional ever comes up with the right idea first time.

# Background work first: what is a radio trail?

Trails are adverts by another name, often referred to as trailers in television or film. A trail promotes another programme on the radio station along the lines of 'looking ahead to tomorrow'. BBC local stations will sometimes broadcast public information trails on road safety and 'don't drink and drive' or perhaps prior to bonfire night, or maybe even water and beach safety. I have recorded beach safety trails with students in the past with a character pretending to use an inflatable toy in the water off the coast. The character gets into difficulty and has to be rescued at the eleventh hour. Students have often made these surprisingly hard-hitting and direct.

## Research

Have a listen to a station that broadcasts adverts. What do you notice about the adverts – how long are they, what do the scripts say, are the adverts funny, how do the adverts make someone do something? In other words, how do they persuade someone to buy a product? The principles apply equally to trails.

## Choose your message, stick to one message per trail

Sometimes the message from a trail is not actually fully written or spoken. Occasionally the message generates an emotion in the audience. For example, you might want to encourage young listeners to buy a dance and R'n'B compilation album from an internet retailer. The trail needs to make them feel that they do not need to struggle into town and search around the shop just to buy a CD. Quickly edited sounds of buses, cars, trains and busy crowds can end with a silent room and a quick tap of keys on a keyboard. Click it, don't queue for it.

## Writing a script

One thought or idea per sentence, because this is not the printed word and the listener does not have the opportunity to go back over the words. Use short sentences. Use everyday words at all times.

Grab the listener's attention at the beginning and make an impression at the end. Keep it to no more than 40 seconds.

## Peer evaluation

Put students into groups and ask them to play back each others trails or commercials. What was the message and was the message clear and easy to understand? In other words, did they get it?

- Does the trail carry the brand name of the radio station or does the commercial carry the brand name of the product or service?
- Does it have the AIDA formula – attract ATTENTION, create INTEREST, stimulate DESIRE, and call to ACTION?
- Has it been recorded and edited properly?

# Geography

Here are a couple of examples of how audio can be used for geography projects. Development as a topic crops up in GCSE Geography in the UK but the subject matter is universal. Here is a classic example of how to use audio in the way described in Diane Lewis' case study, see Chapter 13.

It will take time to organize but the end result can be very powerful and reused for other groups at other times. Here then, is an opportunity to record audio diaries, postcards, features – the title makes no difference – and send that audio between schools across continents to assess the impact of development in different locations. This task will focus on descriptive writing and narrative, along with research and observation skills. This can be a group or individual task.

There is information in the book on how to contact schools in different countries (see Chapter 13). The most obvious contrast would be with a school in the UK, Western Europe or America with a school in an African state. However, what about the comparison of a school in Eastern Europe instead?

What is the level of health care in an eastern European country? Do the public pay for care or is it free? That alone will be of significance to a British student as free advanced health care regardless of age, income and circumstance is seen as a right.

What level of industry dominates the country chosen for this project? Is it antiquated heavy industrial manufacturing or is there still a reliance on farming? Is that modern and mechanized or still based on a large workforce carrying out tasks by hand? How does that compare with a Western technology and banking-based economy?

How does education affect the economy and vice versa? Are there sufficient schools adequately resourced? Is there any evidence of a growing ICT structure?

> ## Task: To record an audio diary on the effect of development on three indicators – health, industry and education
>
> **Outcomes: to understand how development has affected cultures, considering the economic and social impact of development from first-hand accounts**
>
> Clearly there will be a need for research to find a school in a different country or countries to connect to and share information. Some basic research, perhaps suggested by the teacher at this stage, could highlight key points to consider at the chosen countries.
>
> **Extension exercise**
>
> The more able students could include short recorded interviews with local people on specific points – for example, a local doctor on the difficulties of providing free universal health care in a country where scientific breakthroughs and public expectations conflict with ethical
>
>

and financial dilemmas. Closer to home, they could put together an interview with the headteacher on the challenges faced by an education system scrutinized by industry and its needs.

**Differentiation**

Higher ability students could attempt the above quite easily while lower ability students could just record a basic audio postcard – what can they see out their bedroom window, how do they get to school, what jobs do their families have and how do they get to school? To an extent, the project has differentiation built in because it can be approached at varying levels of ability.

Each student now writes an audio postcard script based on the most obvious details of their lives. Where do they go to school, how do they get to school – by car, bus or walking? What are the obvious effects of that decision? Are roads busier at school times and what are the consequences of that?

What jobs do their parents have and where is that employment? What can they see from their bedroom windows – fields and trees or high-rise concrete blocks and motorways?

Experience has shown that although hesitant on the first recording take, many early teen students are more than capable of completing that initial process. Record the audio as described in the recording section in the book (see Chapter 2) and edit on software such as *Audacity* or *Audition*. The sections on editing and mixing audio (see Chapter 3) will help if students want to add further sounds and recorded atmosphere or wildtrack to illustrate their work.

With that completed and the audio saved as an MP3, it will now be possible to email that audio to another school around the corner or around the world. If the school's internet is not up to large files then one of the many free file-sending programmes such as *YouSendIt* will almost certainly be able to handle the task.

Ask the receiving school to do the same and the resulting exchange will bring to life the subject in a way a written exercise alone cannot.

In the UK, Year 9 groups, that is children from 13 to 14 years old, may look at the comparison of two countries. As with the example above, the countries may be one MEDC and one LEDC (more economically developed country, less economically developed country). They will compare key physical and human features, looking at levels of development as with the GCSE project and consider ways in which the countries are changing.

## Volcanoes and earthquakes

Split into groups and divide the groups into victims, rescuers, local politicians and so on. Your news reporter then interviews all concerned using the notes they wrote in the geography lesson. Add to that mix some dramatic news-style music, move from a supposedly studio-based reporter and location teams, and your geography topic will move from the page into an almost real-life situation.

Maybe your group is visiting a particular site – I heard of one recently that visited a very large steelworks. There were plenty of simple interviews with plenty of descriptive background sounds available, edited down and an interesting way to recap the experience or useful later for revision purposes.

# Mathematics

There are a number of quick and simple ways of using audio in the maths classroom. For this subject area, audio is more likely to be used as a tool by the teacher rather than the student. We know it is not a straightforward subject for many students so it is worth exploring any way of helping the message sink in. I was asked recently for help by a Year 11 student who had just failed her mock GCSE maths exam by a fair margin. The 16-year-old girl was left despondent not really knowing how to break the cycle. She wants to do well but she simply cannot remember number sequences or how formulas work once she has left the classroom. So we were about to experiment at the time of writing to see if listening to her teacher, reminding her of formulas and any tricks to remember, would actually work. She was happy with the idea of listening to the teacher's familiar voice at a time when she could best learn; maybe in the evening or early morning in a physical surrounding that helped, away from a potentially stressful situation.

The experiment was straightforward. I asked the teacher to record what was, in effect, a brief series of conversations that could be downloaded to the student's memory stick or flash pen and listened to later. Logically it was decided that if it would help that student, it should be made available to all similar students; students that cannot recall written number patterns from the board.

Remember, this is about putting across sometimes complex information in a way that students can relate to. Formulas are often learnt by going over them again and again and again until it permeates the teenage skull. Not the most rewarding experience sometimes for either teacher or student.

## Task: record the explanation of a formula

Throw in any tricks by way of remembering and keep it short. A recording around two to three minutes long and no longer would be perfect. I have seen this work very effectively with older teenage students but there is no reason to suppose the method cannot be adopted for younger children.

Download audio into digital edit software and edit or top and tail the audio as required. Save as an MP3 or WAV in a computer drive accessible to students and urge them to download the piece onto their flash pens, memory sticks, MP3 players or mobile phones. If there are a few formulas you want to get across, then record or at least save each separately and invite them to download the bundle.

If you feel confident, you could put a reasonably fast-paced music bed underneath, but played quietly, fading out at the end. This is not an attempt to make maths sexy, but merely that much information listened to by young people is often laid on top of a music bed. Listen to the news bulletin of a young person's radio station, for example, and invariably there is music bubbling gently underneath. If you can't face that it will not be the end of the world. The important point is that the students can then take those recordings away with them and listen to them when it is convenient to them. It is a really useful revision tool because they can take part at a time of day when they learn best, in a non-threatening environment and they can still hear your voice. This task has worked best when it is ad-libbed in exactly the same way as the teacher explaining in class. A script sounds forced and laboured and that is the opposite of what we are trying to achieve.

These two-minute audio bursts can be used in class, of course, just to punctuate the lesson. Teachers I have worked with are often surprised at that suggestion. If we are there already, what is the point of playing a recording is the perfectly reasonable question. Simply because the students will listen, guaranteed. It is another texture to the lesson and they are used to receiving information by that means which is why that small piece of accompanying music bed is worth the effort.

This project may seem like stating the obvious because it is so simple, but at least you will know that it works. And with this project in the bag, the principle can be applied to all manner of short class reminders and explanations.

### Task: Record a description of various geometric shapes using the appropriate mathematical language and ask the students to draw that shape from your description

This could be an occasion where a selected student could record the description to play to the class. It will have the bonus of introducing a different voice into the instruction and check the descriptive ability of that student. Why not try a different student describing a different shape. Again, this is a very quick and simple resource that can be used repeatedly. One maths teacher did suggest to me that the obvious answer would be to not mess about with all this and instead video an entire lesson, making it available to watch again later instead. Please don't go there.

An hour-long lesson recorded on one camera from one position on a tripod will not make great viewing no matter how good the lesson was in person. The sound will be awful picked up by the tiny built-in camera microphone, and the video file size will be colossal. To make the lesson interesting, it will need multiple camera angles, therefore repeating parts of the lesson again and again, and at the very least will need a tie pin microphone attached to the teacher. Editing will be time consuming and needs skill. Let's not.

# Some other subject ideas

## History

Audio can take you back to any period of history you choose. Download battle sound effects from the internet and with some straightforward scripting you have World War II or any other war for that matter. The British Industrial Revolution is equally achievable. There are numerous internet sites with sound effects you can download cheaply leaving you to concentrate on the story by interviewing key players from the industrial past or students pretending to be children from that time, working long hours in dangerous conditions. The technical mixing of these sounds is dealt with in Chapter 3.

You can be the fifth Beatle in a piece on the 1960s or an eyewitness to the atrocities of war. As with geography, a class visit to somewhere is a great way to bring revision tasks into to a different arena. Record short interviews at the visiting site with organizers and those taking part, making sure there is plenty of descriptive narrative in there too. Remember to record at least some background sounds, or wildtrack, to create vivid pictures in the minds of the listeners and help them visualize where they were.

## Expressive Arts

The end of term play is an obvious contender. While we are on the subject of battle scenes, I was asked recently to provide a soundscape of World War I for a summer term production. The students were coping with a particularly serious script but it was obvious that there were sections that would prove awkward to get across to the audience without audio. So I created battle scenes from scratch, finding examples of soaring aircraft, guns and cannon from the period and explosions of varying unpleasantness. It ended with the poppy fields of Flanders illustrated by a meadow sound effect of birds and buzzing bees with a distant mix of *A Long Way to Tipperary* way into the background. Interviews with students or even adults in the unseen role of soldiers and generals or possibly the families left at home would lend real weight to the production as their voices played out across a darkened stage.

As an exercise with younger children it would be even simpler to record sounds and get students to mime or create movement to those sounds or to short pieces of interview.

## Technology

Interviews in food technology in the form of conversations with food producers, retailers, market stall holders or even manufacturers in your local area would provide an effective plenary to bring cooking and theory into the context of the world outside the classroom.

## Sports studies

If leaders are good communicators, then we may have one answer by looking at how audio can be used in a project.

Do leadership styles need to vary when considering individual, racket and team activities? Instead of writing an essay, what about recording some thoughts at the time when taking part in those varied disciplines? Take part in badminton doubles and let's get the sounds of the game in that echoey sports hall. Analyse it later by commenting on who makes decisions in the team, about when to go for the shuttle and when to leave alone. Who decides the tactics and why? Is it about a leader and a follower or is there a subtle shift in the relationship of the doubles as the game progresses?

Be the captain in a game of soccer. How should you motivate those players? Is it by nurturing and creating a motivational atmosphere or is it by confrontation and building some aggression to push the team on?

Record these thoughts at the time and follow it up with a few scripted pieces at the end. The hesitant essay on a piece of paper has become an informative, interesting and colourful account of how that student sees themselves. The location sounds are mixed with the location think pieces and the scripted conclusions to create a genuinely interesting three minutes of discussion. Of course some students are happy and excel at written essays, so if that is the right tool for them, then why change anything. All I am suggesting is that if they do struggle, then perhaps audio can help by allowing them to talk and express themselves first, and write later.

Writing an investigation into the structure and functions of the cardiovascular and respiratory systems sounds tricky on paper but, again, even some locally recorded sounds in the school could help lift the piece mixed with quotes from some breathless competitors taking part.

On a simpler level, the students who for whatever reason are not able to take part in the activity of the day could record a commentary of the game. It has to be better than just sitting doing nothing and they will find that being a commentator is somewhat harder than they thought!

## Physics

Not the first area of the curriculum that springs to mind when considering audio, even though we are taking about radio waves and magnetic activities.

A different approach may be needed here so let us put the emphasis back with the teacher. Perhaps there are some points to put across that cannot always be easily answered with a quick experiment or demonstration. Maybe there are explanations sometimes that just have to be the more traditional classroom approach of copying a few paragraphs from a book or from the board. If that is the case then a short *PowerPoint* or *Moviemaker* presentation could help get that message across. Instead of standing by the laptop or computer and talking through the *PowerPoint*, you could record a paragraph or two and insert it into the occasional slide. The audio can be set to play automatically when that slide appears or you click when you are ready. It does not matter that you are in the room; the students will still listen. And of course this can now be a useful resource for another in the department, and used again and again. In *Moviemaker*, produce a timeline of stills and illustrations or maybe a video clip if one is available. Then write or just record an explanation to go with it, adding that audio to the Moviemaker timeline. Save the presentation and leave the WMA file that you have now created on an intranet drive which the students can access to watch later on. They can, of course, download it to a memory stick or MP3 player and use it at home as a revision tool; so for that matter, can your colleagues, who can now pick up the WMA file and save it where they want to for their own lessons. *Moviemaker*, remember, sits there on numerous computers unbeknown to many computer owners. They have never had a reason to look for it until now, and it was there, free of charge, all the time as part of their *Windows* bundle. Produce the resource at home, email it to school or take it in on your MP3. It could not be simpler and teachers of sciences will no doubt be able to think of many such examples where an approach like this could just add that extra lift to a session as a starter or plenary. Resources like this, done well, can take time to produce, there is no denying. Once finished though, they can have a long shelf life and are reasonably easy and very cheap to modify later if needs be.

# Primary schools

If schools are to be, as Professor Stephen Heppell suggests, seductive and engaging places, then we need to remember that these children may be very young but many have exceptional skills before we even get started.

In his case study on equipment (see Chapter 7), Peter Knowles makes the point that teachers should not impose their limitations on children, but provide an environment where children grow creatively using technology that lets their imagination run away.

There are increasing numbers of primary schools that have woken up to that fact and are harnessing some of this inspirational talent. One size does not fit all as we know so there will be some suggestions that some schools just cannot manage for a variety of technical or personal reasons.

As always the sound quality on school websites varies dramatically both in recorded sound and the way it is treated. Beware the microphone popping sounds that can spoil the sound with a mic too close to the mouth. Try a layer of scrap foam wrapped around the microphone if a proper windshield is not available. It is worth a try and I have used that in schools in the past.

Much of what has been written for secondary schools in this chapter can be adapted for primary lessons, but here are just a few additional suggestions including how to create a lesson starter for Key Stage 1 History.

## Audio diaries and blogs

This provides a good place to start for many primary schools. Audio diaries pop up throughout this book because they are incredibly easy to do and have many uses. If a school has a reasonably developed website as opposed to a page, then placing audio on the site is a tremendous way of personalizing the school. For new and prospective parents, there is a real child with their voice explaining something that has happened in the classroom, a highlight of a lesson or maybe a school trip.

Audio diaries could also provide the key to unlock communication for those children that agonize over written work or with specific difficulties such as dyslexia. Let them explain what they have done rather than leave them switched off. A diary could be recorded over a period of time and added to as work progressed, edited later for neatness if required and saved accordingly.

A whole class could take it in turns to record a diary over a school year as a permanent account of what happened looking at all the highs and lows, celebrating the achievements of children.

The school gardening club takes us through the seasons, sports captains tell us about the events, races, matches and medals, and a bike-wise group explains road safety tips to us with relevant dos and don'ts for the road.

These are not just recordings for the sake of it but could be used as part of school or year assemblies. Why not get the older children to record a piece on the dangers of fireworks that are not used safely or the benefits of the walking bus to school?

## Literacy

Teachers can create their own audiobooks as a shared resource across the school or maybe with partnered schools. Read Laura Coppin's case study which features her attempt to write an audio book for a primary class.

Teachers can give children topics or suggestions of how a story should end. For example, '. . . there was home at last, we had made it!' or '. . . and as the night drew in, I was glad it was all over' and '. . . so we'll never know what really happened'. The children can write the story then record onto CD as an archive record of what was achieved. Stories such as these give great opportunities for sound effects and there is plenty of help on how to do that in the edit and mixing sections in this book.

## History

We will take a look at how we can create a starter for a series of lessons on the Great Fire of London topic for Key Stage 1, Year 2 children. How did people in 1666 find out about the fire? If there was a fire in London today, how would people find out about it?

Include sounds of different situations in the recording such as panicking crowds, crackling fires, radio bulletins, ringing bells, people shouting, television sounds, tapping on keyboards and neighing horses. Which of the sounds fit the questions? Where are plenty of sound effects to be located on the internet? If this all sounds complicated and time-consuming, remember a resource like this has a long shelf life.

The teacher records the questions first. They then source the sound effects, saving each sound to a chosen folder in the computer. In an editing software such as *Audacity* or *Audition*, bring each of the edited audio clips onto the timeline leaving a little space so they do not overlap at this stage. It just makes visual reference easier at this stage. Remember this allows you easily to both hear and see the sounds you can capture. Start with the teacher's questions or statements and then the sound effects.

With these on the screen, you may decide now that you want to start with the flames and sounds of panic. Overlap the sounds together so the story begins to take shape (there is more detail on this in Chapter 3). However, as a quick point of reference, whenever you are creating audio such as this, it is important to listen and listen again. It may be necessary to lower or even vary the volume of the crowds against the sound of the fire so we can clearly hear what is going on. That will also help to create a sense of distance with the illusion of people in different places moving in and out of our story. If your chosen audio editing software allows panning across the left and right stereo channels, then here is a great opportunity to have crowds at different positions running around us, even a neighing horse in the old streets of London from the left channel and a ringing bell to the right. Obviously it is not a problem if the facility is not available but it just highlights how a little thought can lift the final product to another level.

We can now introduce the teacher's questions on the timeline either on top of or below the sound effects, fading out the original sounds a little under their voice. When the questions have finished – how did people in 1666 find out about the fire? If there was a fire in London today, how would people find out about it? – add the remaining sounds varying the volume levels but keeping them identifiable to allow the children to recognize and decide the answers.

In a following lesson they could write a couple of sentences each on a particular part of the fire or record a short improvised piece on what it might have been like to be a child in London at the time. If they can manage this, then mix it with the sounds you have already saved to your drive folder.

As a further point, if there are any visiting guests, such as a fire officer talking to the children, then make sure the conversation is recorded or get some older children to interview them and keep that as a resource to be used either to stand alone or part of something else later. (See Chapter 4 for more information on how to record interviews.)

## PSHE or citizenship

In Key Stage 2, Year 3, the topic of Making Friends can be an audio project. Again, we start with some questions or statements. Who is your friend in school? What do people do in school to be your friend? Who is your friend outside school? Imagine someone has just joined your class and school for the first time today and the teacher has asked them to sit at your table next to you. What can you do to be their friend?

Ask the children in small groups to either write their thoughts or preferably just talk through the answers. Record a couple of those part conversations as you go around. If these are recorded on a hard disk recorder, download them before the children have finished via the USB connector into the edit software; play them directly off the whiteboard so the children can hear some of those views. It should provoke more debate and conversation.

## *PowerPoint* and *Moviemaker*

It is possible to add your own audio or the children's audio to a *PowerPoint* presentation. Perhaps the children have created a short *PowerPoint* on *Little Red Riding Hood*. They can add their own voices and help tell the story by placing short audio files on the presentation that can either be clicked with a mouse or can be automatically played when a particular slide appears. Simply:

- Save the edited audio clips in a drive
- In *PowerPoint* click on Insert, then Movies or Sounds from the drop down menu
- Then click Sound from File
- Locate the sound clip you want and single click on that, next clicking OK
- A box will appear on the screen asking if you want the audio to play automatically or when you click on the slide. It is that simple.

*Moviemaker* sits there quietly as a free bundle on countless PCs never to be discovered because the owner never has the reason to look for it. *Moviemaker* is, however, a fantastic tool for the classroom and enables videos, audio, stills and text to be added, creating the impression of a video production. It has some simple and very effective tricks and effects to bring photographs to life. Audio is recorded in the usual way and can be dragged onto a timeline, similar to video editing software packages such as *Premier*.

Novices should fear nothing. It is such a simple programme to use after a modest spell of trial and error; and experience tells me that a great many students have actually found it on home PCs and are pretty accomplished at it. Finished products can be burnt to CDs for presentations or saved as WMA files to be played in class from the PC or laptop, or prepared at home and taken into school on the MP3 player. The work could of course be taken home by children on their MP3 player or memory stick if they have one.

## Special Educational Needs

I have worked with a number of children who find all this something of a challenge. Communication, through no fault of theirs, is not a strong card. Consequently I have tried many different approaches to make sure the ethos of this book, which is inclusive not exclusive, is upheld.

Writing can be almost impossible for some but there are occasions when they must at least have a go. For some children, the writing is difficult but not impossible; it is the reading aloud that grinds to a halt or never really gets started. In this situation I have started by recording what they can do. This is not intended to stress them or make them feel awkward in any way; in fact it helps the celebrations later. With that recorded, I then get them to say just a couple of words at a time and record that, followed by the next two or three words. Often I repeat the words for them showing how to modulate their voice and bring an extra brightness to the words. Back we go to record the next few words and so on, bit by bit. With a few highlights and deletes here and there to take out the gaps, and we have a completed recorded and edited passage. Now play the original piece the child recorded followed by the second version and just watch a smile on their face appear. They know it sounds different and it will be obvious to you. They can take part, they can succeed and they will grow with confidence. It is another simple trick but it works.

## The after-school clubs

Here are a couple of after-school club suggestions; one simple, the other a little more involved depending on available resources. The advantages are quite clear. The projects described below work because we have tried them; young children are far more media-rich than many adults realize; and parents' views and understanding on what schools are about now can be transformed.

It was only a few years ago that I chose to organize an after-school radio club that would take place at a catchment technology college. To start with, it attracted a small but necessary funding stream that paid for a handful of mini-disc recorders and microphones so the project had equipment of its own. Editing of audio could take place on software the college already had installed so that left only a modest supply of paper and a box of mini-discs to buy. The rationale behind the idea was straightforward. A club such as this was unheard of locally so there had been no previous option to take part. It was targeted at Year 5 children in particular which brought measurable benefits in market promotion in an area with dwindling primary school numbers. A project that demonstrated that a catchment school had resources and experience of this kind was excellent PR. It also had the advantage of introducing those young children and their parents to what was potentially their next school, helping to break down those barriers of uncertainty and suspicion.

I then wrote a brief letter with tear-off slip announcing the start of a free after-school club that would last a term if any Year 5 children would like to take part, and duly handed that over to the primary school. I had worked on a maximum of 12 children and wondered whether there would be sufficient interest to scrape them together. When the first 40 replies came back, I wondered whether closing the list would not be a very good idea. The one night a week club became two nights a week to split the numbers and thankfully one or two had to drop out before we started. I was loathe to turn anyone away because there had been no such facility anywhere locally before; it was hard to offer an opportunity only to refuse because their permission slip was a day later than someone else's. A few of my older students volunteered to help which took the project on in another direction. Now, not only were we able to give children their first taste of this technology and way of working, but we were able to encourage older ones to mentor with all the tremendous associated benefits for both sets of students, young and old.

Children will easily research stories on the internet with some support, if the facility is available. Sport is often a safe bet for boys in particular who choose to search out football match reports they can read out as part of a mini-news bulletin. Girls were happy to talk through something that had happened at their school or that was about to happen such as a visiting production, or a school concert, club or sports event.

There is no hard and fast rule here on whether a child is happier with a script or ad-libbing their way through. Experience has shown that a script is the first choice for many. Some are just too self-conscious with a microphone when they feel under the spotlight and others can degenerate into silliness without the clear direction and support a script offers. A mini-radio programme is easily achievable with a group of 9 to 11 year olds like this and, as teachers will testify, an after-school club can be a fun way of learning outside a traditional learning environment. You do not need a radio studio to do this – a computer with free edit software, a recording device such as a mini-disc or hard disc recorder plus a handful of CDs will do it.

I will take you through this step-by-step. Again, this is not the only way to do this; it is a simple method I have used on a few occasions that mirrors fairly closely what happens in the real world.

Split your groups into teams of five or six and offer a series of job roles such as news reporters, entertainment reporters, sports reporters, presenters and producers. The journalists can research their stories happily with supervision if required, while you can help presenters and the producers decide on the real content of the programme. They will need a plan of what will happen during that programme, so the first task is to decide how long that programme will be or can practically be. Fifteen minutes is a long time if most of what you want to do is speech. The average music track though is traditionally around three minutes long so it does not need many to pad it out. These plans are called running orders and it is literally an order of what will happen and when. All professional programmes will use a running order so the presenter hits timings and knows what happens next. So the producer and presenter may want to work on a jingle or ident first for their programme or pretend radio station. That ident – or identity – can just be one name, the Christian names of the presenters or just initials. Many radio stations use one simple, easy to remember word in this market now that is swamped with different stations, so there is no reason why our programme should not follow suit. Remember, the edit software, either paid for or free to download open source, will have effects (see Chapter 3). So our radio station name – ABC – can now have some echo or reverb over the top, with perhaps a tiny segment of tune underneath. A quick edit and we have a jingle or ident that can be included a couple of times. Now we can decide on a music bed. A 'bed' is a piece of instrumental music that plays quietly under voices. It is called a bed because the voice is laid down on top of the bed. Most music radio and even news bulletins these days aimed at a young audience use beds constantly, it is just that we are so used to hearing them these days that we tend not to notice. If a presenter or a news reader talks with no bed then the sound is referred to as 'dry'. It makes a huge difference using a bed and I guarantee that the children will notice the difference because the sound is immediately recognizable as something they have heard somewhere before, even though they cannot be specific. It must be instrumental though; vocals will get in the way and clutter the voices of your presenters, so dance or garage music tends to be a safe bet.

While all this is taking place, the young journalists will, we hope, have found their stories on the internet and can begin writing them up in their own words on computer preferably. The temptation at this point is to write in the most complicated font and in the brightest colour or colours they can find on the computer. Tell them to use either *Comic sans* or *Arial,* or possibly *Tahoma* in black, 12 or 14 point and double-spaced if possible. It just makes it easier to read.

This now has become a useful English task without them realizing because the challenge is to replace words they do not understand with words they do. Reading aloud is hard enough as it is without reading words you do not get. So copy and paste from the internet and re-write the story. Often the story will be long and tedious, far too long for our purposes, so again they may need to edit the story down. Get them to focus on the important parts that the listener needs.

Back to our producer and presenter who can now concentrate on the programme script and running order. We could start with the ident and a quick hello from the presenter and go straight into a tune. After that it is customary for the presenter to read a 'menu' which is simply a list of what is coming up in the programme – 'so in the next hour we will be doing this that and the other'. Even presenters with many, many years of experience will write a menu instead of ad-libbing their way. It sounds tighter and slicker. After that, another tune.

Now we get to the rest of our team. What about some entertainment news at this point? Perhaps there is a brief story in there about a well-known celebrity or something that happened on a reality show on TV last night. After that story, the presenter or anyone else in the 'studio' can take part in a reaction conversation giving their views on what they saw – all ad-libbed at this point of course which introduces a different skill. So in terms of recording, all the voice parts can be recorded one after the other, which is why the running order is important, particularly if you want to announce the name of the tune you have just played or are about to. The music can be dropped in later when mixing everything on the computer and that is all covered in the section on how to mix audio.

Next in comes the news, the sport, the weather, a couple of imaginary requests or maybe a competition and we have a programme. It sounds complicated but in practice it is very simple as long as orders are written down and followed. You could, of course, move a hand held microphone from a CD speaker, back to a presenter, back to the CD speaker and so on to record the programme. But it will not sound anything like as good as already outlined.

The important point is that, if recorded properly, the children will instantly recognize the finished product. They will know that it sounds like real radio and they will be incredibly proud. So in the process we have team building, self-confidence, writing, speaking and listening, IT and peer-mentoring skills enhanced in one package without them realizing.

The second and this time non-internet project can be audio blogs or audio postcards. This has proved very successful with young children who have poor research skills and frankly are not comfortable working their way around a computer. I have used this next project in primary schools in disadvantaged areas where access to any club of this type is usually impossible. All they need to do here is write, or even ad-lib if they have the confidence. I had the idea of audio postcards when working on a project for the Specialist Schools and Academies Trust in the UK.

Imagine a child was writing an ordinary postcard to a friend that lived in a country elsewhere. This postcard was perhaps the first correspondence so it introduced the child to their new friend. They wrote about who they were and what they did. Let us now convert that into an audio postcard instead. Using spoken rather than written word, get the children to tell the story of who they are and where they are from. What can they see from their bedroom window? Tower blocks, a car park, fields and trees? What do they do when they come home from school, play with friends, and watch TV? How do they get to school? Do they walk or go by bus or car and how far away is school from their home? What food do they eat and what is their favourite meal? This is all very obvious material, but tell the children that they are writing this for a child who lives in a country totally different to theirs. So the child receiving the audio postcard may be astonished to hear they did not walk 10 miles to get to school or fetch fresh water. They may be surprised that they ate cereals and milk for breakfast and had a cooked meal in the middle of the day and could not possibly imagine what a chicken nugget was. A project such as this is simple to do because the material is to hand and it helps celebrate the child and their community. What goes into the postcard is personal preference. It may focus on that school, that housing estate, a project happening nearby; anything that helps the child take a look at their community and where they are from.

Each child writes and then records their own postcards. They can listen to each others, offering feedback. There is a real opportunity to involve parents here to by getting them to take part on the postcard, offering their own opinion after their child's. It may be one simple task but here we have the beginnings of school as community. It provides a vehicle for shared experiences, contrasting experiences, reflections and opinions, and it could provide a chance to get parents actively involved in something taking place at the school that is positive and has purpose.

Once recorded and edited, transfer the audio to a CD and keep at the school as a record of what took place. There would be advantages in repeating next year or maybe twice a year and build up a record or archive of how the community developed over time.

The audio blog is all but the same of course with a slightly different approach in style and content. The blog is a diary or audio column and the children could record what happened to them this week, something they want to get off their chest or details of an event taking place. There maybe is someone technically able at your school to put those blogs on the schools intranet so they could be accessed and played back in all classes encouraging more children – or even staff –to take part. This then again moves away from being merely an after-school club and becomes part of the culture of expression and confidence where children write or speak, use IT, consider values and beliefs, have respect for differing opinions and believe that, actually, they do have something to say themselves after all.

In the example of the after-school club it is worth noting that rarely did a child miss a planned session and even then it was only due to exceptional circumstances, and of course, this was purely voluntary as far as they were concerned and at no financial cost to parents. Parents were not directly involved in that project, but it was noticeable that many made a point of actively finding the rooms where the project was taking place and stood around the rooms or craned their necks through doors. They could have waited outside the building, of course, in the otherwise empty car park with no other children around. However, it was clear talking to some mothers that the project was the big talking point for many of the children. It had become extremely important to them. The parents then had a real curiosity about what it was that had so encouraged their child, coupled with a fascination for the technology and concept that had so attracted their young son or daughter. There were plenty of 'there was nothing like this when I was at school' conversations to be had and some were genuinely surprised that something like this could be done in the first place.

Parents then had a sense of transformation of their reference points for school and learning taking a huge shift sideways. Suddenly, their thinking and judgements were challenged and they had the opportunity to wonder what else may be different. It also crucially gave them an opportunity to be inquisitive about a project that mattered to their child, to be wrapped up in their enthusiasm and certainly in some cases to wish that they too could take part in some way. Other parents found themselves on the back foot with their under-12 child in the driving seat, outlining what amounts to an example of media literacy to them. The child was the leader and the project connected, and all that from one simple idea.

## Public relations

Not so obvious perhaps but immensely valuable. As mentioned earlier, the interview on the website with a successful sports team can only give a good impression. Add to that a brief piece with the headteacher or principal edited down, with questions removed if necessary.

There could be very short interviews or even vox pops with students on departmental pages of the website – real people, real students talking about why they enjoy those subjects. A series of interviews or vox pops with Year 7 students edited together and placed on the homepage will produce an excellent introduction for Year 6 children looking to move the following year. The students can tell both the younger ones and their parents what the first few months were really like and that the move is not as confusing as they perhaps imagine it to be. That school switch is traumatic enough for parents and children, so what better way than to hear those who have just made that move tell of their experiences: audio that can be heard whenever it is convenient to those families. It is invaluable public relations in what can be in some areas a tough student recruitment marketplace.

There are many more examples and it is not long before every area of the curriculum can be covered in some way. The answer is invariably yes before asking the question. Remember this need not be a single-handed operation – colleagues can help. The advantage is that these resources are then available for as long as you choose to use them. Updating audio like this is also a relatively simple operation once the main resource has been produced.

In the following chapter, you can find sample schemes of work that are easy to adapt to suit a given project, regardless of subject or qualification.

# 6 Sample schemes of work and worksheets

This chapter contains two schemes of work that can be adapted as a template across the curriculum and for a variety of ages. To start somewhere, the schemes have been written for two BTEC Media projects. The idea and principle behind them could be adapted for the forthcoming Creative and Media Diploma Lines; for example, the Year 10 scheme on producing radio news bulletins and commercials could be modified for the proposed diploma module titled Campaign. Commercial production fits squarely in the Campaign unit to promote a service or product.

The Year 10 scheme and topic could also be altered to suit an English lesson, looking at the power of words and how they can motivate the public to do something they had not intended or to create awareness of a situation. Such a topic can also be used to introduce the spoken word script or modified to produce public information trails on a range of seasonal situations from drink-driving at Christmas to water safety in the summer. This task really focuses on the use of words and how every word must be made to count. See also Chapter 5 for help on producing trails.

The point is simply to use these schemes as templates: get an idea that fits the subject and be creative. The tasks consider ideas and planning followed by production time then evaluation from teacher and peers. The schemes are followed by two worksheets that look at the rapidly changing circumstances around a train crash. Although originally intended as a task for young journalism students, the idea can be modified for other subjects as the introduction to the worksheets explains.

# Scheme of Work – Year 10

| Title: Radio Commercials/News Bulletins | | | | Start date: September | Tutors: Mki |
|---|---|---|---|---|---|
| Subject: BTEC Unit 5 Audio Production | | | | | Group: Year 10 |

| | Topic | Aim | Methods | Resources | Assessment | Evaluation |
|---|---|---|---|---|---|---|
| **Session 1** | What is Media? Design a music magazine masthead | To understand more about what the term 'media industry' means and assess what the student already knows | *Moviemaker* presentation, Q/A and handout | *Moviemaker*, projector, board, handout | Q/A to establish prior knowledge followed by unaided project to assess understanding | Whether prior knowledge exists through initial practical and level of feedback and Q/A. Homework: complete planning |
| **Session 2** | Music masthead | Produce unaided masthead design on computer. To understand how to use colours and text to create an image and attract an audience | Students' work unaided on final masthead design to determine prior skills levels | PCs *Photoshop/Publisher* | What skills students have by producing a design unaided on PC | Skills levels without teacher input at this stage – can they use software and have an understanding of basic codes and conventions? |
| **Session 3** | Produce an audio product | To listen to audio and understand why it has been produced in a given way | Listen to radio examples. Students work in pairs to make notes on what is appealing to an audience. Discuss radio ads | PCs, internet, paper | Whether students have any understanding via Q/A of what appeals to different age groups | Written notes produced. Homework: write a proposal 300 words for chosen project |
| **Session 4** | Produce a radio commercial Produce a radio news bulletin | To be able to select news appropriate for a target audience/ news/sport for a 16/24 audience. To be able to come up with words and sounds to create an ad image | Students work in groups or individually to decide content. Research news stories on internet, copy/ paste | PCs internet, software recording device, radio online | Whether students can research and produce ideas fit for purpose | Group plenary, whether ideas work and can be recorded convincingly Differentiation: produce ideas for a campaign of two or more ads but record one. Consider a feature idea |

*Sounds Like A Good Idea* © Mike Kinnaird (Continuum 2008)

| Session | | | | | | |
|---|---|---|---|---|---|---|
| **Session 5** | Produce a radio commercial<br>Produce a radio news bulletin | To be able to rewrite top news/sport stories of the day in spoken word for a 16/24 audience.<br>To be able to write words and sounds to create an ad image | Students work in groups or individually to decide content. Research, make notes | PCs, internet | Whether student can follow on from research and source suggestions | Whether students can confidently make suggestions and plan scripts.<br>Homework: complete at least one plan |
| **Session 6** | Produce a radio commercial<br>Produce a radio news bulletin | To be able to rewrite top news/sport stories of the day for a 16/24 audience in spoken word.<br>To be able to write words and sounds to create an ad image | Students work in groups or individually to decide content. Write scripts, research audio effects, try recording | PCs, edit software, paper recording device | 1–2–1 Q/A and self-assessment | By observation – ability to write unaided on PC as part of team or individually. Test ideas using recording device and software. Student self-assessment.<br>Homework: complete a script/plan/running order |
| **Session 7** | Produce a radio commercial<br>Produce a radio news bulletin | To be able to record product | Record scripts individually or as a team. (Other design projects if waiting for equipment) | PCs, edit software, paper recording device | 1–2–1 Q/A and self-assessment | Rewrite and/or re-edit and teams listen to another's to offer peer assessment<br>Differentiation: complete a design project if completed |
| **Session 8** | Complete edit and evaluate | To be able to record and edit audio effectively. Self/peer assess own skills | Listen to other students' work if possible then self-assess | PCs handouts | 1–2–1 Q/A and self-assessment | Whether students can assess own skills and suggest improvements.<br>Homework: differentiation as above |
| | REVERSE PROJECTS AND BEGIN THE SECOND CHOICE AS ABOVE | | | | | |

*Sounds Like A Good Idea* © Mike Kinnaird (Continuum 2008)

| Session | | | | | | |
|---|---|---|---|---|---|---|
| Session 9 | Produce a radio commercial / Produce a radio news bulletin | To be able to select news appropriate for a target audience/ news/sport for a 16/24 audience. To be able to come up with words and sounds to create an ad image | Students work in groups or individually to decide content. Research, make notes | PCs, internet, software recording device, radio online | Whether students can research and produce ideas fit for purpose | Group plenary, whether ideas work and can be recorded convincingly |
| Session 10 | Produce a radio commercial / Produce a radio news bulletin | To be able to rewrite top stories of the day in spoken word for news/sport for a 16/24 audience. To be able to write words and sounds to create an ad image | Students work in groups or individually to decide content. Research, make notes | PCs, internet | Whether student can follow on from research and source suggestions | Whether student can confidently make suggestions and plan scripts Homework: complete at least one plan. |
| Session 11 | Produce a radio commercial / Produce a radio news bulletin | To be able to rewrite top stories of the day in spoken word for news/sport for a 16/24 audience. To be able to write words and sounds to create an ad image | Students work in groups or individually to decide content. Write scripts, research audio effects, try recording | PCs, edit software, paper recording device | 1–2–1 Q/A and self-assessment | By observation – ability to write unaided on PC as part of team or individually. Test ideas using recording device and software. Student self/peer assessment. Homework: complete a script/plan/running order |
| Session 12 | Produce a radio commercial / Produce a radio news bulletin | To be able to record product | Record scripts individually or as a team. (Other design projects if waiting for equipment) | PCs, edit software, paper recording device | 1–2–1 Q/A and self-assessment | Rewrite and/or re-edit and teams listen to another's to offer peer assessment |
| Session 13 | Complete edit and evaluate | To be able to record and edit audio effectively. Self/peer assess own skills. | Listen to other students work if possible then self-assess | PCs, handouts | 1–2–1 Q/A and self-assessment | Whether students can assess own skills and suggest improvements. |

*Sounds Like A Good Idea* © Mike Kinnaird (Continuum 2008)

# Scheme of Work – Year 11

Title: Audio book plus poster for Year 3 primary children  
Start date: September  
Tutors: Mki

Subject: BTEC Unit 17 Media Production Project  
Group: Year 11

| | Topic | Aim | Methods | Resources | Assessment | Evaluation |
|---|---|---|---|---|---|---|
| **Week 1** | Introduce topic . . . . design a media product of own choice | To research, plan and produce a media product using available resources and skills | Moviemaker presentation, Q/A and handout. Self-assessment. Prepare/proposal document legal and ethical considerations | Moviemaker, projector, board, skills audit handout | Self-assessment of skills audit | Whether skills audit has been logically completed |
| **Week 2** | Research plus homework | To research possible product based on original ideas | Research audio books on internet, compiling notes/advantages/disadvantages | Internet (if none, group discussion, team work) | Observation of research outcomes | Homework: continue/complete initial research |
| **Week 3** | Research or prepare a proposal | To settle on an idea(s) to be developed | Finalise a written proposal or note form and devise a pitch for the product. Tasks to be completed, roles/team working strategies/logistics/clearances/risk assessments. Develop: research/viability/audience/draft scripts/thumbnails/storyboards/production schedule | PCs, paper, workbooks, recording device | Completion of tasks/group plenary / Would a primary teacher use this book? Is language appropriate for chosen age group? | Notes produced, exercise completed via Q/A |
| **Week 4** | Develop a proposal | To outline precisely what the product is and the audience it will serve | Finalize a written proposal or note form and devise a pitch for the product. Tasks to be completed, roles/team working strategies/logistics/clearances/risk assessments. Develop: research/viability/audience/draft scripts/thumbnails/storyboards/production schedule | PCs, paper, workbooks, recording device | What have I done? What do I need to do? | Homework: what are the risk assessments needed for two products, to be identified |

*Sounds Like A Good Idea* © Mike Kinnaird (Continuum 2008)

| Week | | | | | | |
|---|---|---|---|---|---|---|
| **Week 5** | Make a product | Produce the product according to the proposal | Write audio book script, proofread Qualities: technical appropriate to medium. | PCs, software, cameras, studio, etc | Self-assessment notes | Optional homework for differentiation. Produce one additional element of the product, e.g. script lines or alternative image research |
| **Week 6** | Make product | Produce the product according to the proposal | Show book script to primary teacher for feedback and assessment to assess language/style/content. Record test piece. Source images for accompanying poster create images. Qualities: technical appropriate to medium. SAVE ALL WORK AND/OR PRINT OFF AT THIS STAGE TO SHOW PROGRESSION | PCs software, cameras, studio etc | Self-assessment notes | Optional homework for differentiation. Produce one additional element of the product, e.g. script lines or alternative image research |
| **Week 7** | Make product | Produce the product according to the proposal | Re-write script, record audio. Qualities: technical appropriate to medium. SAVE ALL WORK AND/OR PRINT OFF AT THIS STAGE TO SHOW PROGRESSION | PCs, internet, paper | Group Q/A to determine where we are and any peer support | Optional homework for differentiation. Produce one additional element of the product eg script lines or alternative image research |
| **Week 8** | Make product | Produce the product according to the proposal | Edit audio, complete image manipulation of poster/cross-check against proposal document. SAVE ALL WORK AND/OR PRINT OFF AT THIS STAGE TO SHOW PROGRESSION | PCs, internet, software recording device etc | Cross-check against proposal | Plenary: what existing products are now like my product? Who would watch/read/buy it? How do I know? |

*Sounds Like A Good Idea* © Mike Kinnaird (Continuum 2008)

| Week | | | | | Give work to peer for assessment | Effectiveness of peer assessment |
|---|---|---|---|---|---|---|
| Week 9 | Make product | Complete the product | Complete recording and poster layouts/edits and print. SAVE ALL WORK AND/OR PRINT OFF AT THIS STAGE TO SHOW PROGRESSION. | PCs, internet, software, recording device, etc | Give work to peer for assessment | Effectiveness of peer assessment Homework: initial thoughts for evaluation (300 words) |
| Week 10 | Evaluation | Different evaluation methods | Test audiobook recording on primary teacher/and class, feedback from teacher and children. Compare with original proposal, appropriateness to audience, look at technical qualities, pre-production: research, planning, time management, and creative abilities, own work, team work. | PCs, internet, recording device | 1–2–1 Q/A | 1–2–1 Q/A |
| Week 11 | Evaluation | Complete evaluation | As above plus: production logs, comments from peers, teacher, audience, etc | PCs, internet, recording device | Checklist assessment 1–2–1 Q/A | 1–2–1 Q/A |
| Week 12 | Evaluation Hand in completed project | Complete evaluation | As above plus: production logs, comments from peers, teacher, audience, etc | PCs, internet, recording device | Met deadline | Met deadline |

*Sounds Like A Good Idea* © Mike Kinnaird (Continuum 2008)

# Worksheets

## Extension exercise: The train crash and other situations

Without getting into a debate on the rights and wrongs of the spoken word over the written word, here is one simple example of how the spoken word can be introduced into English or media lessons, and add a sense of pace at the same time.

Indeed the principle can be adapted for other subjects. Take out train crash and substitute earthquake for geography (see also lesson ideas in Chapter 5). The students then write a short radio news bulletin about the immediate effects of the quake with updated details to follow including quotes from some of those involved.

In modern foreign languages ask the older, more experienced students to write about a planned day out, perhaps to the seaside or a theme park. Then introduce a problem; tell them the day is cancelled because someone is ill, the weather is bad, the car has broken down. The point of this exercise is the change of information under a deadline. It has worked in almost all cases in the past. However, through trial and error with groups and students of varying ability I have now tended to use this as an extension exercise. It has worked just as well with mid-teen students as with older students, even adults in some cases. Indeed some of the mid-teens have produced more engaging results than the adults.

I originally wrote the train crash version to use with NVQ 4 Broadcast Journalism students, then adapted it for much younger BTEC students. Hand them the first worksheet making it quite clear that the information will be updated in 20 minutes or so. Major news incidents are always unclear at the beginning as details trickle through. Having been in this situation so many times before as a journalist I am only too well aware that emergency services have far better things to do then talk to journalists when a major incident occurs, and quite right too. They are there to save lives, not meet a news deadline.

Not surprisingly, details can be contradictory, vague and even, as in the case of the first Train Crash worksheet, legally unstable. The 'deliberately negligent' line was originally intended to see if the older potential journalism students had even a basic awareness of defamation. However, when I adapted the material for the younger student I decided to leave the line in just to see what happened. I confess to being pleasantly surprised that in almost every case, the 14- or 15-year-old student spotted the problem in many cases straightaway or after the smallest of hints. It was at least as successful as with the adult student. This was not intended to be a gimmick but to show them a little taste of what it is really like out there in the real world and the consequences of getting it wrong.

Ask students to write a quick radio news bulletin piece on the crash as they know it, now bearing in mind that immediacy is the key. So 'a train crashed earlier today/a short time ago', rather than at 7.30 which can time date the piece. Also remind students that they can't use direct quotes on the radio. In other words they can't read out loud

'A spokesperson for Bancroftshire Police, Inspector Terry Jones, said, "Details are still sketchy but it's clear we have a major incident". They should write instead something like 'Inspector Terry Jones of Bancroftshire Police says (pronounced sez) this is clearly a major incident. But he admits details are still sketchy'. Not much of a change but it is the way it is done.

After 20 to 30 minutes, hand out Worksheet 2 and ask students to rewrite the story from scratch based on the new information. With 10 minutes left, get the group or selected students together to talk through the pieces, asking a couple to read out loud to assess whether it sounds like radio news or someone reading from a newspaper. They will be able to hear the difference.

Next session, record the bulletin pieces as required, downloaded to the students' individual screens and using the edit software, get them to add underneath a news bed piece of music that you have already provided to create a bulletin item.

Write another piece, create a news jingle and on it goes.


It may seem a great deal of trouble for not a great deal of work produced, but the students do enjoy the pace of it. They gain a deeper understanding of how all this works and pick up new transferable skills along the way.

# Train Crash 1

## BTEC Audio Unit

This is a *fictional* news story to simulate the pressure of a real newsroom.

**Task:** To write a radio news story based on this press release

**Lesson objectives:** To be able to write a radio news story in the spoken word under rapidly changing circumstances

IMPORTANT: There is a legal problem in this copy. If you read it out loud it could be a serious problem for you as a journalist. Can you spot it?

## News Release

### Train Crash near Bancroft

At 7.30 this morning, a train crashed between Bancroft and Tadminster. It's believed the crash site is around 10 miles out of the city.

The emergency services say there are a number of injuries but the exact number is not known. Bancroft Fire and Rescue estimates there may be as many as 10 seriously hurt and two fatalities but the Bancroftshire Ambulance Service says reports from the scene indicate there could be many more dead. Ambulance crews have only recently arrived.

The commuter train to Caddington left Bancroft Central Station at 7.25 and it's thought it was full of passengers, possibly up to 150 people.

Passengers at the scene have alleged that an additional 30 to 40 people many have been standing. They say all those injured and dead were passengers without seats. They said the train operator, Target Trains is negligent and deliberately let the train leave knowing full well passengers were at risk of serious injury.

A spokesperson for Bancroftshire Police, Insp Terry Jones said, 'Details are still sketchy but it's clear we have a major incident. Colleagues from British Transport Police will lead the investigation along with and Health and Safety officials. We can't say how or why the train left the rails yet but we can't rule out vandalism of the track. Obviously we would wish to extend our sympathies to the families of the dead and injured.'

### Note to Editors:

Target Trains is one of the largest providers of passenger transport in mainland Europe.

Target operates two rail franchises in the UK – Target Trains Scotland, a commuter rail network, and Target Trains Northern which provides urban and inter-city passenger rail services across the North of England.

Names of places and those involved are fictional for publication purposes.

# Train Crash 2

## BTEC Audio Unit

This is a *fictional* news story to simulate the pressure of a real newsroom.

**Task:** To write a radio news story based on this press release

**Lesson objectives:** To be able to write a radio news story in the spoken word under rapidly changing circumstances

## News Release

### Update on Serious Train Crash

Officials are still at the scene of a train crash near Bancroft today. The 7.25 from Bancroft to Caddington left the rails 15 miles out of the city near Tadminster. Ambulance crews have taken 22 seriously injured passengers to hospitals across Bancroftshire. Bancroft County Hospital announced it was activating its Major Incident Procedure and brought extra staff in to cope with the incident.

A spokesman for Bancroftshire Police Insp Terry Jones said, 'We believe quite clearly now that vandalism was the cause. Eyewitnesses have reported seeing two youths and one man dragging what they say were large logs and a metal trolley of some sort onto the tracks.'

Insp. Jones says the tragedy was compounded by the fact that the derailment happened at the fastest part of the journey.

The train operator, Target Trains, says it deeply regrets the tragedy and says its teams will cooperate fully with any investigation.

Emergency services have confirmed that six people were killed. Five were pronounced dead at the scene and another died later in hospital.

### Note to Editors:

Target Trains is one of the largest providers of passenger transport in mainland Europe.

Target operates two rail franchises in the UK – Target Trains Scotland a commuter rail network and Target Trains Northern which provides urban and inter-city passenger rail services across the North of England.

Names of places and those involved are fictional for publication purposes.

# Part 3

## Case Studies

# An introduction

The case studies in this section feature those that have used audio successfully in the classroom or the community. They cover what equipment to buy, what not to buy and consider how young people use audio, media techniques and social networking skills that teachers can tap into.

This section begins with Peter Knowles, the Managing Director of *Total Audio*, one of the many equipment suppliers that are used to dealing with the education market. This case study covers advice ranging from school radio installations to simple voice recording in the classroom and microphone selection. Peter outlines the need for schools to know what they are trying to achieve before they buy any equipment and the need to concentrate on file-based audio, finally leaving tape behind. He discusses how school radio stations must operate on industry lines and offer credible skills demanded by employers.

Dr Guy Starkey is Associate Dean (Media) at the University of Sunderland. He is one of the UK's leading media academics and has written several course-specific media books. Radio is his specialist theme: 'Just give [*students*] the means of using audio and show them what to do and they will be inspired'. In his case study, Guy outlines support available for non-media teachers who find themselves with the school media portfolio; with a view to bringing teachers and teacher training centres onboard, he points out that students are already creating high-level audio products in their private lives.

Teachers are producing inspiring activities in the classroom but they need support to develop further and not criticism, says Dr Jan Robertson, Director of the London Centre for Leadership and Learning. Jan outlines how she began using audio herself as a means of helping students catch up or recap on her lectures. Her case study illustrates how she made audio diaries for the Specialist School and Academies Trust website following a tour of the UK meeting education leaders. She also considers student demand for interactive ways of learning and using students to build resources as best practice.

An audio project that connects a secondary school with a local primary is outlined in Laura Coppin's case study. Laura was a 16-year-old media student but wanted to produce a genuine audiobook for young primary children. Her study goes through the process of how the idea was developed and the changes to language and direction that had to follow. A discussion with a teacher at a primary school looked like ending the project before it had been completed, until a last minute idea for literacy lessons came to light.

Professor John West-Burnham is in demand worldwide as a leading authority on school leadership in his role as coordinator of the European School Leadership Project. John considers why teachers should look more closely at the media skills already inherent in their students and why teacher-training centres should encourage the media-rich skills that trainee teachers already use in their private lives. He looks at the connection between the use of audio and social capital and audio as a means to create extended learning rather than an extended school.

Heat Rays 87.8 FM was a short-term FM radio station run on several occasions by Monks' Dyke Technology College in Lincolnshire. The practicalities of running a high-end use of audio in a school is detailed in the Heat Rays case study. It was a radio service for teenagers by teenagers. The case study recalls how and why students were involved at the very beginning including the choice of name, how programmes were produced, why training is crucial to the successful outcome along with input from radio professionals and a few hints on how to engage the local press in raising awareness and the ultimate prize of bridging the community.

Diane Lewis is Director of Instructional Technology, Seminole County Public Schools in Florida. She leads numerous schools around Orlando in the quest to use emerging technologies in the most efficient way. We look at a joint project between Diane and a school in the UK to assess how students view the choice of technologies before them and how or why they use them. Diane's case study outlines various options for schools looking to connect with schools outside their country.

Robin Webber-Jones is Curriculum Manager for Media at South Leicestershire College and is a Director of the not-for-profit company, Crystal Clear Creators, for which he was a founder member. He has compiled The Leicester Experience which looks at a number of stories from the city which have used audio to re-engage students for some time. Kimberley's story shows how she came to use audio and how audio brought a group of students together that had found themselves on the edge of the curriculum and the traditional learning experience.

My own case study concludes this part of the book.

Sound is what makes great audio; words are not enough. Words can tell of a situation but it is sound that involves us in the same way that video engages the television news audience. I recall my search earlier in my career for a distinctive sound that would engage an audience. If I want to record a piece with a local retailer for business studies or maybe the town mayor for citizenship, then let's record them in the High Street. Why find the quietest room available when we can use the everyday sounds around us to help tell the story?

The case studies give an overview of how students are already leading from the front as significant users and producers of audio and other broadcast-based content without necessarily realizing it; they give an overview of students' roles as sophisticated social networkers and consider how teachers can lock into that. The case studies address the most important point of all: producing audio is just great fun.

# Peter Knowles: What equipment to buy and what not to buy

# 7

*Peter Knowles*
*Managing Director of Total Audio Solutions, Bromsgrove, Worcestershire, UK*

## It's all about compromise

*Total Audio Solutions* was set up as a professional audio facilities company in 1996 by ex-broadcast *Sound Supervisors*. It provides its services to schools, universities and colleges but also to broadcasters, location sound recordists, post-production studios, outside broadcast facilities, theatres and PA companies.

The main points featured in this case study are:

- Do not buy anything until you know what you want to achieve with students; buy equipment with students in mind, not teachers.
- Know what equipment you do not need
- Recognize that band PA equipment and radio studio equipment are not the same
- Ask reputable suppliers for references and follow them up
- Advice on which microphones, headphones and recording devices to consider
- Record all audio as digital audio files
- Operate school radio stations on industry lines and offer credible skills demanded by employers
- Share skills among teachers

Traditional broadcasting is not having the best of times at the moment as budgets for equipment in the highly-competitive digital age get severely squeezed. So not surprisingly there are increasing numbers of suppliers positioning themselves towards the booming education market. As with all sectors, there are some suppliers who seem to take delight in ripping off schools because they are easy targets. However, there are far more that fully support the ethos of schools moving into comparatively sophisticated media areas and are delighted to help and advise. Peter Knowles is a highly experienced sound engineer with simple and effective advice for schools that find themselves able to enter the world of audio in the classroom, particularly radio. He has worked on a long list of flagship BBC programmes and continues to provide audio facilities at the highest levels; equally he is happy to help a school with plenty of ambition but a tiny budget. Peter's company is just one of many out there who can offer practical support.

The following case study was based on a recorded interview.

Peter's first and possibly most important piece of advice is the most obvious. If you have a budget (particularly a large slab of public grant funding) to invest in a studio, always but always ask a supplier for references. A supplier with any credibility will be able to offer references from satisfied customers. Ask for references from schools that have set up similar projects in the past. It goes without saying that you should chase the references up.

Peter is most frequently asked about radio studios as more and more schools dip into the market: 'The question is usually "What sort of studio should we buy?" And my reply is always "what do you want to do with it?"'

It is possible to buy radio station studio packages – everything that a school would need initially, including equipment and studio furniture – for under £10,000. Some of these starter deals are particularly good. It is possible to spend even less of that grant funding and still build a useful facility.

As Peter says: 'I believe, in this situation, many teachers are like islands. There doesn't seem to be any central way of communicating with each other. They have the same needs and the same problems and what they really need is support. Teachers do seem to think that they have to go out and do the whole thing themselves but there are people to help. So often they have an idea and want to get on but don't actually know what it is they are trying to achieve as an end result.'

There is a temptation to buy something that looks good and to buy equipment that they do not need. A common problem, according to Peter, is that teachers will often buy what they are familiar with, so they might end up with equipment that is far too domestic or it is far more akin to music and band use.

'What usually happens is that they take advice from a music teacher or maybe they have a friend in a band. Equipment for music PA or mixing is not for radio.

I think radio is the perfect medium; it's a level medium. You don't need to be able to play an instrument or look beautiful; you just need something to say. That's why radio in education is such a great format.'

'But how many people know how to record or edit?' asks Peter. How do you transmit it, how do you get on the web?

'All this is straightforward, to be honest, but if no one has shown you, you can end up completely on the wrong track.'

So the starting point should be what do you want to do with the studio? Once that has been determined, the next critical element is to build a facility that is relevant to the outside world and to jobs, which only underlines, says Peter, the need to avoid the band PA route and the need to buy equipment specifically for radio.

Peter believes it is very important that young people gaining experience from the school studio use equipment and develop skills that are wanted and needed by employers.

'When students leave your course and go to that local radio station looking for work or to continue their education elsewhere, they need the right skills. If it is not relevant, then don't bother to do radio at all. They must operate in the same way that industry operates and develop an understanding of why something is done in a particular way.'

Training, says Peter, is critical, and he returns to the idea of relevance. Peter maintains there is no point in giving students a big flash studio if no one at the school has any idea how to use it properly. It is very easy to put in a solution that is too big, too complicated and too expensive.

'There is no point in us installing equipment that can't be used otherwise we will get phone calls every day, so an assessment of available skills is crucial. A studio for the sake of it has no value.'

And with a note of caution, bear in mind that those skills may be held by just one teacher in a school. When that teacher leaves, there could be a serious problem as the teacher leaves with those skills.

Now to a more basic level of voice-recording in a classroom with reporter packs. First thing's first: forget about tape once and for all. Even mini-discs, seen by some as the next best alternative, have in many ways had their day. The way people use audio in their private lives now blends seamlessly into broadcast and audio technology. It is the file system of audio that should be the first choice for schools, according to Peter – by that he means hard disks.

'The future isn't film, it's digital and the future isn't tape, it's file-based. I learned how to edit on a two-track machine at the BBC, and you still hear people saying that tape editing is the best way to get experience. But that's gone. You give a nine year old a computer and watch them fly it ten times faster than we can. Give them a new phone and within minutes they know everything it can do. We're still reading the manual.'

So the next piece of crucial advice is to not to buy equipment with a teacher in mind. When schools buy equipment based on a teacher's perspective and not the students', the students realize the limitations of what that equipment can do and what they achieve as a result, and rapidly lose interest. They need to be able to go further and try more complex projects to develop their creativity and understanding. It some ways this echoes the requirements for a studio; the need to buy equipment that is simple to use but has the option of additional skills and challenges later.

## File-based audio

As Peter points out, once a piece of audio has been saved on a hard disk recorder of some sort, that audio can be used and sent on in a variety of ways. This interview with Peter was, for example, recorded with a microphone and telephone set-up plugged straight into a computer. The audio was then recorded and saved on *Adobe Audition*. This means it can then be opened on a computer as a *Windows Media Player* file. Digital audio files like this can then be emailed, saved to CD or DVD, saved on a memory stick, even on your phone if you have a USB socket on your phone.

'If you use any other system, like mini-discs for example, you will only have to convert to a file later anyway to be able to use it with today's technology.'

As for specific manufacturers of hand-held reporter-style recorders, there is another word of warning, with one eye on the High Street. Don't just buy the familiar domestic equipment names. Peter recommends an American company *Sound Devices* and *Fostex* and *Tascam*. The *Samson* 'Zoom' hard disk recorder series that record as MP3 or WAV are also highly recommended by some and are very affordable. These are not domestic equipment manufacturers but are specific to the industry market.

## Microphones

What is Peter's recommendation for microphones to be used for the heavy-handed 14 year old?

'There is an argument that says you should spend as much as you can on microphones. Admittedly, the sound you record is as good as it gets, so a poor quality microphone equals a poor sound. But there are still some cheap and really quite good hand-held mics out there. *Audio Technica* make some at under £35 and they're great.'

Peter points out that hand-held microphones work well in schools because they are usually tough and can take some handling. They can deal with wind and breath noise well.

He suggests avoiding condenser microphones: they pick up too much of everything and can sound horrible in the wrong hands. However, different microphones do different things; they are not all the same.

So the next question, says Peter, is perhaps from a music teacher who says he wants to record some music, or expressive arts who would like a production recorded. In that scenario, the hand-held mic that operates at 18 inches from a mouth at its limit is of little use. In these cases, it is much better to invest in a gun mic, sometimes referred to as a rifle mic. Rifle mics are so-called because they record what they are aimed at, rather like a gun, and tend not to pick up additional sounds at the sides. They are usually long, thin and pointy.

Three gun microphones in a row along a stage would pick up what was needed.

There are some general stereo microphones available but tend to be limited in what they can do. The general advice according to Peter is to stick to a simple hand-held mic that is affordable and can do a variety of tasks, whilst accepting that they cannot do everything. Cost and all round versatility are the factors here with a nod towards compromise.

With a final word on microphones, Peter discussed the current trend in certain quarters for USB microphones – microphones that plug straight into a PC or laptop via a USB port. His conclusion was that it is still early days for the technology which smacks of gimmick and is of limited value at this stage. It is far easier to take a hand-held digital hard disk recorder than trudge around with a laptop to record the audio on.

The mantra on microphones is that you can achieve far more with a cheap microphone used properly than with an expensive microphone used badly.

## Headphones

So to headphones. Broadcasters in the age of super-sensitive health and safety have jumped on to the headphone situation. Industry tends now to issue staff with their own personal headphones rather than let people share this thing that clamps around a variety of different ears, hair and skin. At a push, employers will issue wipes to allow the next person to give the spongy ear cups a good wipe around.

'In education, this has never really been addressed', states Peter. 'Certainly at university level, I would want to know what my audio really sounds like with a pair of headphones that I like. I would want my own and not share. But in a school with a class of 14 year olds, that's just not practical.'

As for manufacturers, he suggests looking at the industry stalwart, *Sennheiser*. Whatever the manufacturer though, the best advice is buy rugged, or 'National Health' as Peter describes it, rather than delicate and spindly.

The reasons why are obvious; rugged will last, so do not be tempted to buy on pretty looks alone. Peter also points out that, of course, the expensive pair of headphones are the ones most likely to be borrowed permanently. If that is the case, the money was wasted anyway.

So sound quality should not be the number one priority for schools, it is all about durability and cost in the classroom. For the school radio station, however, spend that bit more on both the headphones and microphones because the overall quality bar is higher there anyway and they are more of a permanent fixture.

## A professional approach

If the school studio looks professional, then experience suggests students as a rule respect that far more. Equipment taken out of a box and stuck on a table looks like what it is. Equipment in the studio that is built into custom furniture creates the right impression.

'Straight away, students feel this is a great place and we are on air, we are recording,' adds Peter.

## Loudspeakers

The final topic of conversation is loudspeakers, referred to commonly as monitors in industry. It is possible to get 80 per cent of what you want with a modest cost. It is the last 20 percent that bumps up the price by a huge jump, and for schools that just is not worth it. So again this is another piece of kit cloaked in compromise. There are plenty of very good quality speakers on the market that cost substantially less than even three or four years ago. Again *Fostex* and also *Tannoy* are names to watch for the studio at less than £200 a pair. Monitors of that quality will really allow students to hear exactly what they have recorded with remarkable clarity and that is more than good enough. As before, the next step up is a very big step and just not worth the cash for schools.

Peter's recommendations are clear:

- Ask for and follow up references, make sure the reputable supplier knows what it is you want to achieve.
- As a teacher, do not buy equipment that is in-line with your own limitations but equipment that is right for the job at a cost you can afford and equipment which will give students the opportunity to really create and stretch their learning experiences.
- The equipment needs to grow with the students; so much equipment now has plug-ins that are additional facilities and software that can be downloaded onto the recording devices, often free of charge – the digital equipment that you bought continues to evolve.
- Training is key. Find some relevant industry-based training for staff. Make sure the knowledge is shared and that there is a fallback position – 'I come across this all the time; schools left with kit they suddenly can't use properly because no one thought to make sure the skills were shared. Take advice and think it through.'

On a final note: 'The good news is that today equipment is affordable and it is possible to get great results comparatively easily. Just spend carefully and remember that if a school wants a studio, don't spend all the money on a flash building and top class equipment and then forget the acoustics. Equally don't spend £80,000 on acoustics and have no money left for equipment. It's all about balance and need.'

# Guy Starkey: Using radio to inspire and re-engage students

**8**

*Dr Guy Starkey*
*Acting Associate Dean (Media), School of Arts, Design, Media & Culture, University of Sunderland*

## There is some fantastic work out there.

Dr Guy Starkey is one of radio's leading academics. He is widely published with numerous practical course textbooks to his credit. He is also involved in developing curricula, student support materials and assessment instruments for national qualifications, including Higher National Diplomas and National Diplomas. He has also researched a number of different aspects of the media industries, in the United Kingdom and abroad.

The main points featured in this case study are:

- Video should not always be considered as the first choice
- Radio can be used to inspire students
- Students can produce audio that sounds like a professional product
- Avoid expensive acoustic treatment when old blankets and curtains will do the job
- School intranet radio versus RSL FM radio projects
- Support available for non-media teachers who find themselves with the school media portfolio
- Students are already creating high-level audio products in their private lives.

This case study was based on a recorded interview.

'Across the curriculum, radio can be used to inspire students; it's that simple,' is the opening comment from Guy Starkey. Although he clearly spends a great deal of his time running a busy university department, Guy is very much on the pulse of media techniques in the classroom. He is known up and down the country as a course moderator and textbook writer.

During our chat late one afternoon there were a couple of significant points that drifted into the spotlight. Why is video the dominant choice of most teachers when such projects have a nasty habit of going spectacularly wrong? Can radio be used to bring disenchanted students back into the fold?

Radio, as we have discovered throughout this book, is a credible choice for teachers looking to widen their repertoire of teaching methods. It wins every time in terms of cost and ease of implementation. And we also know now that the students are half way there with their own skills base as kings of the download and all things web.

'Just give them the means of using audio and show them what to do and they will be inspired,' says Guy. 'Cheap video work usually looks naff. Compared to the professional product, cheap or amateur video tends to be worlds apart, and there's hour after hour of this on video-sharing websites like YouTube to back that up. But by following the simple rules, it is much easier with audio to get a professional sounding product. And the only thing I think that kids will be sensitive to when making audio products is the sound of their own voices; they're conscious of what they sound like. Young lads whose voices haven't broken yet can be very aware when listening back and can be a bit uncomfortable. But we can work with that and if they get mixed together with different young people on joint projects across the curriculum, that problem usually goes away.'

With radio an increasingly hot topic in many schools, the question of short-term FM radio licences, or RSLs, usually rears its head at some stage (see Chapter 1). An RSL can run into many thousands of pounds which puts it beyond the average school budget and into the funding arena. However, as Guy suggests, there is always a Plan B.

'RSLs are great if you have the funds and the confidence to do that. I did my first at Farnborough in 1992, but you don't always have to do that. Why not, for example, just send a feed of your radio programming to a social area in a school? You still get radio without all the costs of a fully blown RSL.'

It may well be possible, for example, to use the school's intranet to send audio from a computer in the studio to a laptop connected to speaker cabinets in the school canteen.

On the subject of money, Guy also points out that expensive acoustic treatment in school studio areas is not always necessary when egg boxes and old curtains or blankets draped on walls will also do the trick.

Back then to the topic of media techniques in the classroom and Guy acknowledges that many teachers are exploring ways of using these skills to bring subjects alive.

'I know many teachers are already doing great things in the classroom and using media techniques because obviously I see what my own children bring home,' he says. 'But teachers usually opt for a print-based approach. They tend to go for the magazine or the flyer format.

'So they get kids researching a topic and then produce a magazine or a newspaper on what happened to Oliver Cromwell for example. And they get little stories together. So some are already conceiving of using media techniques to inspire kids to engage with work, but they are not considering radio as an alternative way of telling the story.'

And so often the answer is simply that the option never occurred to them and no one has shown them how to do it.

As we said a moment ago, video is so often the first choice from the digital toolbox for many teachers. Almost every teacher has had a go at making a home video at some point – a child's birthday party or the family holiday.

'So what do they do? They say "right, kids, let's make a video" and on it goes from there, and they probably can't conceive of how radio programmes are made or audio products generally,' suggests Guy. And of course the huge file size is a problem with video. Things are much easier with audio, there is less likelihood that the computer will crash like it often does with video. So I really support the idea that we should be encouraging more teachers to consider radio in the classroom; even encourage them as a starting point to listen to more podcasts to appreciate the benefits a little more.'

Teachers who have tried video productions in the past may well at this point be nodding heads ruefully as they remember the number of times the PC crashed under the strain of gigantic video files; the not-so-very pleasant experiences of watching valuable coursework evaporate into the ether yet again.

This predominance of video is not a situation exclusive to the non-media classroom though. Within media as a subject, there is also an overwhelming taste for video as a number one choice.

Looking across different centres that teach the National Diploma in Media, it is possible to see that there are a far greater proportion of people doing the moving image pathway than the audio pathway. As Guy Starkey suggests, it is highly likely that centres teaching the National Diploma are exclusively offering the moving image pathway, without any opportunity to even consider audio.

'Because of course when you are recruiting students for your centre, you steer students to areas which you think are the strengths of your department. Looking through various prospectuses you are bound to find the moving image is predominant, which is a shame.'

This train of thought then led us to talk about the teacher who was landed one September with the school's media portfolio. Media as a subject has been seen by many in recent years as a fairly generous cash cow and a useful income stream. Unfortunately, the person elected for this new, shiny and high-profile role is often an English teacher or performing arts specialist with no experience of media whatsoever. While the spread of media is only likely to be encouraged within the pages of this publication, what can we do to support the now startled non-media teacher left blinking in the headlights of a subject that they nothing about?

Guy quickly pointed out that there was in fact a fairly generous supply of information out there: 'I have certainly formed an opinion through my contacts and working with schools that a number of teachers have had media landed upon them. And it's perhaps not the most comfortable subject matter they have had to deal with.'

The media exam awarding bodies offer reasonable quantities of INSET support in a number of ways. Teachers can go to publicized INSET training days that are usually listed on the exam board websites; or they can ask for training to be given on site.

'Edexcel will, for example,' according to Guy, 'find out what teachers' needs are and will then give them a training event onsite. There is also another source of support from a website called *mediateachers.co.uk*, and that has information for precisely this kind of situation that some teachers face.'

There are also exam specific textbooks on the market for teachers taking media classes with plenty of hints and tips and photocopiable materials.

We next touched on a subject also covered in Professor John West Burnham's case study (see Chapter 11). Not all teacher-training colleges seem to be enthusiastic followers of the digital options available. Many young trainee teachers will have had no time or instruction on the use of current media practices in the classroom. Colleges will say there is no time in the syllabus. However, Guy Starkey says he thinks it is a real shame.

'I have been thinking back to teacher training many years ago when overhead projectors and slides were innovations. The people who led those sessions were very keen and enthusiastic and young trainee teachers were exposed to that. Now, I am not sure that young teachers have a wide repertoire of skills that modern media technologies will allow. It's just a shame that what is advocated within this book is not standard fare on teacher training courses.'

So what about young people themselves, how are they likely to react to radio, or audio if you prefer, arriving unannounced into the classroom? Is audio just a bit low-tech now? Television is undoubtedly sexy when compared with radio, a point not lost on those of us that have worked in the industry. Radio though, has undergone a colossal makeover in terms of content, style, accessibility and platforms for delivery. Anyone with microphone and a PC can take part in an internet radio station from home and, as already discussed elsewhere on these pages, listening to the radio on a mobile phone is now relatively commonplace.

Evidence suggests that young people do like radio in its increasingly varied forms – a small miracle when considering the absolute lack of interest shown by the established broadcasters in the UK that have turned their backs on children. A presentation from Guy to the Radio Studies Network Conference in the summer of 2007 outlined his views on the dismal level of children's radio. He reminded the audience of radio professionals and academics about the dire predictions often repeated that young people were turning their backs on radio and audience figures will progressively fall. However, research into audience listening patterns is something of a strong point for Guy which enables him with some conviction to state that those predictions are almost certainly wrong.

'What has happened of course is that radio as an industry has done very little to encourage children. There is no national children's network. There is children's programming through CBeebies on BBC7; three hours on a Sunday afternoon for example from 2pm, but that is very much a niche service at only certain times of the day. Whereas in terms of children's television from 7am until 7pm there are two non-stop BBC children's television networks with other commercial channels available. Radio just has not looked after children and the BBC and commercial radio should be ashamed.'

Commercial radio many years ago had dedicated children's weekend programming but, again, sadly no more. Radio does, however, expect young audiences to join the fold and support its services as Guy points out. 'Radio One, for example, does nothing for children now but they expect that, at the age of 15, young people will go to them. Commercial radio expects, at the age of 18, young people will go to them, but there is no encouragement for parents to sit and listen to the radio with their kids as used to happen 20 or 30 years ago.'

However, the democratization of audio now means that those young audiences are taking matters into their own hands and creating a parallel service where they set the agenda and content.

'My 13-year-old daughter is very resistant to the idea that she should turn out like her dad in any way at all. But actually, when she got a laptop and I gave her a copy of *Audacity* (see page 32), she discovered that she could record her own voice and process it; make it sound funny, in fact do all kinds of things with it. Now she really took to this and I said to her that she was just like me. I told her that I used to make recordings on a tape recorder in my bedroom when I was her age.' – a suggestion that was naturally rejected out of hand as any parent will appreciate.

But to come full circle, Guy reiterated the point that, given the tools and the opportunity, children will be inspired and they will make it their own.

# 9 Jan Robertson: Teachers like practical ideas

*Dr Jan Robertson*
*Director of the London Centre for Leadership and Learning*

## Teachers like ideas

Dr Jan Robertson was recently appointed Director of the London Centre for Leadership and Learning following a highly successful role as Associate Professor and Assistant Dean in the School of Education at the University of Waikato, Hamilton, New Zealand. She is internationally regarded for her work on coaching and mentoring. Her book *Coaching Leadership: Building educational leadership capacity through coaching partnerships* was the basis for a number of workshops across the UK for the Specialist Schools and Academies Trust.

The main points featured in this case study are:

- Use voice clips to enhance presentations
- Podcasting lessons and lectures
- Students demand interactive ways of learning
- Students build resources as best practice
- The use of mobile phones to connect with students effectively
- Teachers need support to use available technology
- Advice for those with no experience on how to create audio diaries for websites
- Creation of audio diaries by distance learning using personalized audio tutorials and emails.

This case study was based on a recorded interview.

Let us be clear about one point. Jan will be the first to say that there is fantastic work already taking place in schools. In fact at her own centre lectures are now offered as podcasts. What is suggested here is that the outlook is very positive but teachers need support not criticism; they need someone to lead and show them just what can be achieved from harnessing some media technologies. Jan realized that audio had a very useful place in her repertoire many years ago. As an internationally renowned speaker, she is in great demand across the world for her workshops and seminars. During those many presentations, it became apparent to her that audiences enjoyed the experience of hearing recorded voice clips in those sessions to illustrate specific points. It gave another dimension and added a different layer to the message she was putting across. So if this was a presentation on coaching, for example, here was a clip with a headteacher with his or her own take on what Jan was saying; it brought the presentation to life. Simple enough, but with a huge impact.

Jan would be asked after a session: 'What can we listen to later, in a month's time, in the car on the way home?'

'So what I did for my Master's teaching was I podcast every class I took. Literally [I] put a tape recorder on and recorded the class and made a resource like that,' she said. The students found it incredibly valuable. It was that success that prompted Jan to think seriously about audio as a quick and easy, but highly effective, tool.

'It was there that my commitment to the electronic world started, of how people can access in their own time, can go back to information. And I think we have just got to embrace it.'

Every teacher everywhere knows how tricky it can be to motivate everyone in that room, so did those students actually go back to those lessons?

Yes they did. 'I was quite surprised,' confesses Jan. She points out there was no compulsion but she did tell the students that she was interested to know how they used the recorded lessons if indeed they did.

The majority of the class did go back to the recordings of the lessons; they enjoyed putting them onto their MP3 players; these were people often in mid-career too, so they were not necessarily the next generation of MP3 users. They were the 'digital immigrants', so to speak. Jan says the students were thrilled that they could easily catch up on a session if they missed something and they enjoyed the process of listening on demand.

But there are some teachers, I suggested, who will say, this is all well and good but here I am being asked to produce yet more resources for my class and I just have not got the time. How do we persuade people that are really under time pressure that there is an absolute benefit from something like this?

'I think there are two or three ways we can approach this,' Jan countered. 'One is we can show people that this can build into a useable resource that can last for many more times and used in many more ways. Often people's nervousness means, and I can speak for myself here, that it is a little daunting and a little threatening because of not knowing about the technology or about how to do this quickly. So it's making sure there is support and peer support for that sort of thing to happen. Also I think many teachers will look positively at this when they realize students are demanding materials because they are looking for interactive or reflective ways or connected ways of learning.'

As Jan points out, when some research is completed on how students embrace technology and how it is impacting on their learning and achievement, then that is when teachers will react positively. When teachers can actually see for themselves that it is going to make a difference to student engagement and student achievement, then many more will bite the bullet. That is when they will say they are not too busy.

I suggested next we consider that student at the back of class who feels there is nothing in this for them. It is not the lesson particularly or the curriculum subject. It is just that the way he or she is being communicated to has no relevance whatsoever. Jan's response was that with the UK government's stated policy of personalization, audio does allow the student to pick and choose from a large global resource: what they need to know more of, hear more of, and go into in more depth, by doing more self-directed study. She has anecdotal evidence that the use of mobile phone text messages from headteachers to secondary school students has been a powerful way of engaging them in the school. This view allowed me to reflect on how many headteachers had banned mobile phones altogether in schools. A lost, or more accurately perhaps, a misread opportunity?

Basically, Jan feels that in this digital world we can be learning from young people. She recounted a situation were she was talking to a class of 9 year olds. She asked, 'What would happen if we put a web cam in every classroom? What would we be able to use them for?' The list of ideas that these very young children came up with was absolutely wonderful in terms of how they could use this resource to enhance learning.

So this should not necessarily be seen as something that only teachers have to do. This can be a powerful learning experience created by those young people. For example, if a teacher has a topic on worms in biology, let the students get on with making the audio clips. Let the students create and build up the resources that can be used again the following year as best practice.

I suggested that this is an example where the teacher is mentor and the group is one unit: teacher and students together, all moving forward simultaneously. It is also about trust. As Jan has said elsewhere at one of her presentations, trust is the basis for open, critically reflective relationships. It will also lead to combined ownership of the process.

No one suggests for a moment that any of this is easy. We all know the apocryphal tales of the 5 year old who can programme the video recorder while the parents are still poring over the instruction manual. It shifts power from teacher to student and there are some who are not confident or comfortable with that. Some years ago I remember discussing some audio work I was doing with a senior academic leader who suggested that some of my ideas were a bit too soon at the time because so many teachers still struggled with email, never mind anything else. Times have, of course, changed.

The thrust of Jan's argument is that it is simply not good enough to tell teachers to get on with it. It is not reasonable to expect people to adapt to and adopt new ways of producing resources without leading them first. Put simply, you have to know what you are doing or how can you be expected to take part. Agreed, we may well be familiar with a range of resources at home from MP3 players onwards; the questions are how to use them in the classroom and how to integrate the approach across a school. If there is no integrated approach, the divide between popular and unpopular subjects widens. We can use MP3 players and mobile phones in our last lesson but you can't in this one . . . The message is confused; it builds in resentment and conflict, and for what purpose?

Much of Jan's current work is about showing teachers how to become partners in the learning relationship, and that, she believes, is one of the most important steps. Teachers, sitting alongside their students, asking what it is about their computer games that keeps them engaged. What resources have you found on the web, how could we use some of our digital resources such as web cams, audio recorders and the internet to make learning more exciting? Ask them directly, what would you do? Get them to be part of the process.

But let's not get too dismissive here. There are increasing numbers of teachers out there who do not find it at all threatening and who do wonderful things. So Jan says, don't take me to the lowest common denominator; take me to the ones that are doing these great things and let's start celebrating that. The trick, of course, is not just to celebrate but to share, whether that is sharing with colleagues, the education cluster and/or the community. The added value becomes tangible.

Jan would like to see, and can imagine, great benefit in a detailed researched look at how some teachers are using emerging technologies to enhance achievement and the assessment of students' responses to how their way of learning has changed because teachers have used technology – or, as I suggested, how students have used technology to help each other.

In other words, with a continuing shift towards peer mentors and coaches, there are plenty of young people there to guide teachers in the technology while the teacher focuses on the information to be delivered; both student and teacher take on different roles as coach but with a common aim. Surely that level of partnership working can only be beneficial?

With the interview now drawing to a close, we considered for a while the newly qualified teacher. He or she has probably had little or no time to consider this as part of a training module but here is the perfect example of a young person already immersed in the world of technology in their private life.

Jan's reply was that to say to the young teacher to get on and use technology in your classroom would be a wasted breath. Jan would want to lead from the front and show first with practical advice; to demonstrate the power and to show exciting technology can be. This is not about doing someone's job for them; it is about supporting and enabling someone to reflect on what is possible, how it would work and how to build that creative culture. That would be the most important point; these young teachers must always engage with young people in the worlds in which they live.

But, Jan cautioned, this approach does take a skilled practitioner; it takes someone who can guide a group around various sets of resources, someone not afraid to utilize the skills within a group, someone who can ask the students who is best at using this equipment. And of course, as she points out, while all this is happening, teachers get ideas and that is what teachers like – ideas.

So the more we can find where this is new practice is happening, the more teachers can see these ideas brought out at conferences, workshops and seminars– that's when we will see a take-up.

## Coaching Jan by the click of a mouse. Testing, one, two.

During a brief conversation with Jan Robertson towards the end of 2006, it became clear she was a keen supporter of using audio in the classroom. At that time she was in the UK in her capacity as Associate Professor at the University of Waikato. An in-demand world authority, she was here for the Specialist Schools and Academies Trust (SSAT), leading workshops right across Britain under the banner, *Rethinking Pastoral*. The events were designed to enable and encourage school leaders to question their pastoral systems and drive forward changes within the context of the UK's *Every Child Matters* agenda so that personalizing learning is achieved. The trust asked me to help Jan record some audio diaries of her experiences, thoughts and reactions as the workshops unfolded.

Although this part was a new experience for her, the idea at least gave Jan the chance to vocalize her thoughts and to reflect after the event. I recommended some basic, simple but high-quality recording equipment for the Trust to loan to Jan for her stay over the coming months. It was important to get the best sound quality available because the aim was to edit the diaries down to manageable chunks and place them on the Trust's website. There were two options: either I visited Jan at every venue and recorded the conversations, coaching and guiding her through the recordings, or I helped her remotely. The second option seemed the sensible answer for two reasons: there was the cost factor both in travelling to each venue and time spent; and arguably though, the more important point, was that Jan would not have got as much out of the experience if I had been there. I can record interviews and bites of speeches and workshops standing on my head. Far better surely, for her to have a go at recording herself, to learn new skills both in recording and interviewing and cascade those skills later to others back in New Zealand. Of course, we were not to know that Jan would soon be packing a case, or several cases for that matter, and move half way around the world to live and work in London. Not only was it cost-effective to get Jan to do the recordings herself, it had the potential to provide a set of transferable skills that she could use again and encourage others to use. And that surely is the point of all this.

As mentioned earlier in this book, I spent 20 years in total at the BBC where sharing skills with the outside world was a very silly idea indeed. Without going over old ground, the equipment was ferociously complicated at the back end of the 1970s and into the 80s and letting the outside world loose on that kit was not even a discussion. Consequently, the skills were jealously guarded, kept in-house and the community gained nothing in that sense.

Here with Jan then was one simple project where she could not only lead her inspirational workshops in person, but could create the means where she could share those concepts and reflections, and those of others, to anyone at anytime, anywhere at the click of a mouse. She did not need me there; she needed support to enable her to complete the task to a standard she felt was appropriate and representative.

Once recorded, the raw audio was emailed to me so I could listen and provide feedback. Some of that audio was off-mic, with a sprinkling of loud closing doors, I seem to remember, creeping in at one conference. I recorded tutorials for her after listening to that audio, offering tips on how to avoid some problems next time, tips on simple things such as mic rattle, popping and off-mic voices. That audio was then emailed to Jan and we completed the process with phone calls, when possible, and texts. But the advantage of this yo-yo audio email was that we could pick it up, of course, when it was convenient.

By the way; here's one small piece of advice at this point. When sending that audio, make sure it is as an MP3 and not the monstrously larger WAV file. I am so used to working in WAV to maintain the highest possible sound quality that I accidentally sent Jan a WAV tutorial on one occasion. It was the equivalent of sending a wardrobe through the post instead of an envelope and it was an unpleasant experience all round for the poor laptop holding onto its hard drive for dear life, trying to cope with such a gigantic file.

So there was no need to meet face-to-face.

This is the critical part of this example. I could help Jan with specific audio tutorials that she could listen to at her leisure. She could then send me fascinating diaries and interviews that I edited and mixed with a couple of my own links within the time frame but at a time that suited us. No need for a classroom, no need to be in the same town or city. To extend that, there would be no need to be in the same country or continent. I really do want to shout this from the rooftops. Face to face is a crucial element of many learning experiences, but it need not be the only way. In the glorious days of 1960s black and white television and trade test transmissions, I clearly remember watching mind-numbingly dull BBC schools' broadcasts while nursing measles or some other inflammation. The BBC began TV for schools on September 19, 1960 after two years of planning. Radio broadcasts to schools go back to 1924, almost the birth of the BBC; so distance learning using emerging technologies is hardly new.

The audio diaries duly appeared on the SSAT website for all those unable to attend one of those sessions. They appeared as a five-part series, each package around three minutes long. So for example, one part featured a headteacher who described how the innovative philosophy and culture in his school led to working with students to develop a new rewards programme. Another was a discussion with a number of educators about how pastoral care relates to other aspects of the personalizing learning agenda. At my last visit to the Trust's iNet site, the diaries were still there.

Whether Jan had been in the same building or across continents the end result would have been the same. Is this the global village we hear so much about, is the world flat after all?

The next logical step in the process, which we were not able to complete, with Jan's move to the UK, would have been to demonstrate to her how to edit her own audio effectively. With those skills in place, the learner is then coach. They can pass the complete package on to the next person, helping, nurturing and advising and calling back on occasion for additional top-up or advanced skills. So the first person in the chain does not need to run themselves into the ground and yet the one-to-one learning and coaching continues apace. It is not just something that happens to you but a collaborative experience. The story starts all over again.

# Laura Coppin: An audio liaison project between primary and secondary schools

## 10

*Laura Coppin*
*Sixteen-year-old student taking a BTEC media course as part of a range of studies at Monks' Dyke Technology College in Louth, Lincolnshire*

*Sadie Davison*
*A Year 3 teacher at Kidgate Primary School in Louth*

The main points featured in this case study are:

- How to produce an audio book
- Cooperation between secondary and primary school pupils and staff
- Audiobook as a BTEC audio coursework project
- The use of language skills when targeted at a given audience
- Audiobooks with a cliff hanger as an aid to literacy lessons
- The use of varied voices when producing products for young children
- Primary children as audiobook authors swapping stories across towns and countries for completion
- Audio as a means of creative writing, speaking and listening, IT, teacher CPD, sharing best practice and shared resource-building with a long shelf life.

This case study is based on a recorded interview.

## An audiobook produced for a primary school class by a secondary school student

Laura was a typical school media student who slowly but surely grew before your eyes with confidence and skills. The ideas were there already. All she needed was a vehicle with which to express herself. For this piece of course work, she wanted to produce an audiobook. Although this was a BTEC coursework project, the principle is adaptable in many ways, not just for young children. Indeed, other students have since adopted the concept for audio stories aimed at much older students; this is also a useful idea for primary teachers to take on board. However, that was never the intention. As with so many creative ideas it is so often the spin-off that is particularly gratifying.

For this unit of her BTEC, Laura could have chosen anything at all. The brief is as open as it is simple; just make a media product, be that print, audio, video or web. It does, as with any media project, require research and planning, something students are rarely keen on. Boys in particular want to cut out the middle stage and get straight to the computer. Computers are interesting and they do things, whatever that is. Drawing on a piece of paper is not quite so attractive and, of course, it is easy to see why.

A great many girls, though, are happily engaged with a piece of paper and a pack of crayons, producing detailed and highly colourful planning sheets. They may well be improbable ideas but, nevertheless, excellent ideas to work with and develop.

Laura had already had some audio experience on radio projects elsewhere in her BTEC course. She was perfectly fine with print-based materials but producing a front cover and a double-page spread for a magazine of her invention and all the planning that went with it did not really punch her buttons.

So after a page or so of initial ideas and scribbling she condensed this down to an audiobook, something neither she or anyone else in her group, had attempted before.

To keep Laura's print skills going we decided to complement the book with a poster or graphic of some of the characters in the book, but at this stage the idea was nothing more than that.

As a vocational qualification – and the same will apply to the new Creative and Media Diploma Line to be introduced in the UK from September 2008 – a sense of realism and industry awareness is a key issue. Students should realize, even from this age that a good idea is only a good idea if someone wants to buy it.

This unit requires a student to consider ethics, copyright, intellectual property and target audiences. It expects that a student will produce detailed planning, storyboards, roughs and all the necessary research, and of course a product pitch. The pitch appears later in the UK's A level Media qualification, so for the student looking to progress this is a useful exercise.

To add some realism to Laura's project, we agreed that it would be valid research to take her draft script to a nearby primary school and get her story checked by a teacher who knows what very young children will like. The aim was to produce a short audiobook that could be burnt to CD initially and played to a real class; real clients in other words that could make or break the success of the idea. Initially, Laura had a 5-year-old child in her mind when devising the idea, but would the language she used be appropriate, would the children understand what she had written and would the story have any relevance to a child of that age? Should there be a moral to the story or a message, or should it just be plain entertainment? Would she write a story that would inadvertently upset or frighten a five year old? Would they even sit through an audiobook or is this already old hat and out of date? Should it be a single narrator or multiple voices and what about the balance of male and female voices; do very young children react better to some and not others?

A great many questions to answer which began with a story that Laura entitled *When Molly Lost her Kitten*.

> One morning Molly wakes up to find that her kitten is nowhere to be found. She looks everywhere she can think of, from the park to the pond to the big oak tree. During her search, Molly meets all her animal friends – a dog, a duck and a bird – and they join in the search. But it is all in vain and the kitten is nowhere to be found. Molly goes home only to find that her kitten was there all the time. A tried and tested formula, then, of introducing new characters through the story, keeping a sense of anticipation going, culminating with a happy ending.

Laura said she remembered stories from her young childhood where animals featured strongly and could talk. She took a second draft to Sadie Davison, a teacher of Year 3 children who are 7 and 8 years old. She chose a little girl as a main character assuming that young children would associate with a girl more strongly and gave her the name Molly for no other reason that it sounded cute. At this stage, prior to meeting Sadie at the primary school for the first time, everything was purely guesswork. This included the secondary idea of a poster. Again, prior to this first meeting, Laura decided the poster would in fact be a graphic of some sort that would include all the characters. Rather than a poster intended to sell or promote the audiobook, it would be used to display on a screen or whiteboard from a projector, to give the children a focus while listening to the story.

Sadie's initial reaction was that the story was in line with what she was reading to her class; talking animals for example, and the language was appropriate for Year 3 children. She said was trying to imagine the voices these characters had as she read through and that those voices would be important to the success of the book.

Even at this early stage then, Laura was faced with some realities. She had a 5 year old in her mind when writing the story but the language was closer to a 7 or 8 year old. That may not at first seem an issue but the two-year age difference is a matter of understanding or not understanding the story: that would have an impact should this be a commercial product. There was also the fact that the voices used, or the way the voices interpreted words, would be of some significance. As an audio product, this was a fundamental point.

The animal friends all needed names, rather than just 'Bird' or 'Duck', so somehow those names required introduction. According to Sadie, her children get very attached to the characters if they have a name which increases their involvement. Any particular names, something short and easy to remember? Sadie did not think so, but some alliteration would be useful, so Brian the Bird and Daisy the Duck would help.

Back to the language. Sadie suggests this would be better for 7 year olds rather than 5 year olds. Was it the language generally, or any particular meanings or perhaps a combination of words in a sentence? For example, 'wandering about' – Sadie said she had noticed that the kitten was perhaps 'wandering about' in the first reading and suggested 'walking about' would be better.

Small details perhaps but if we are producing valid audio products for a classroom then this is the level of detail to be considered.

Laura could quite happily have continued this project without ever stepping into a primary classroom. She could have made the audiobook without ever consulting a primary teacher. But for the sake of a thirty-minute session, she was now armed with real feedback, real information that would take her project into a different league. There were still questions to answer as we will find out, but the plan now was to re-write with audio instructions and produce this so it could be played in Sadie's classroom as soon as it was practical.

I asked Sadie about audiobooks in general – have they any place? Sadie's response was that it is very useful for children to be able to hear someone different telling the story. They listen and they enjoy the story but when you put on different voices they know it is you and they know it is you trying to make it more enjoyable for them. They just do not find it quite as enjoyable as listening to a different voice, making those voices. I asked if a male or a female voice was better. She replied that she had not heard an audio book with a male voice but that was perhaps down to the books she had chosen rather than the fact that a man's voice was less appropriate.

With those points now taken on board, it was back to Laura's story. Is there anything else that needs consideration was the next question.

Sadie delivered the killer blow.

'Sorry, despite everything we have said, I don't think this is a particularly engrossing story, certainly for my children in my class. It is a very short story and I do not think it would grip them.'

Laura's project was unravelling with every sentence. Sadie did say, however, that they would be interested in what happened to the kitten. There was a happy ending to Laura's story and the children liked happy endings, but nothing much happened in between. Perhaps a rescue of some sort, was a suggestion – they like adventure and excitement.

But if the character was in danger and had to be rescued, would that not be too much? Apparently not.

I do remember, like many of my baby-boomer generation, hiding behind the sofa while trying to watch BBC1 on a Saturday night. There was William Hartnell in *Dr Who* narrowly missing extermination yet again from Daleks or some other chap who was apparently a monster from another universe but in reality dressed in a boiler suit garnished with various bits of plastic pipe. So maybe some good old-fashioned scary bits were fine after all. Children have a different view of fear to adults. As a child a piece of fear can be exciting: as a child I happily sat in a cable car way up in the air at a holiday camp. Now I think twice about tackling a step-ladder without a risk assessment.

The book Sadie is reading in class at the moment has some scary characters in it and the children were really excited. The good characters are in danger in parts and she says she makes sure she stops at some of those good parts. They want to hear more. They listen and they want to make sure the character is safe and they get very involved with it. It was at this point in our interview that a life raft for the project drifted into view.

Clearly children like a cliff-hanger and some excitement was not only possible but desirable. Would it work if short stories like this were to be a starter, an introduction to a story that ended abruptly at a crucial point? Definitely. So children could then listen to the audio story and pick up the story themselves? This, suggested Sadie, would be perfect for literacy lessons, leave the story open without any clues and let the children use their imagination to work out a written conclusion.

So using audio in this way would be a valid way of engaging the child's imagination. Initially this would happen by allowing them to hear a story, characters, sounds and voices to build this world in their minds and then asking them to complete the scenario. That would tackle their listening skills, creativity and writing skills in one go. That, according to Sadie, would be far, far better than giving the children a text of a story on the interactive whiteboard.

There is a further important point here. Sadie suggests that a combination of audio prior to writing could also have a positive access impact on lower ability children. Expecting teachers to find time to pen literary masterworks in their spare time is hardly realistic. However, writing short starters like this, particularly as a Key Stage team or as part of a parallel group, or in the role of coordinators, becomes more manageable. Remember, these stories need not date. So as with all products like this, the time-consuming part is at the front end but the resource can have a substantial shelf life, rolled out again and again. Those schools working as a cluster could also share such products emailed back and forth building up a considerable library of time-saving resources. Especially, as pointed out by Sadie, if there were different story settings. So perhaps there could be a horror story, an everyday setting, like the missing kitten saga, and an action adventure. Other year groups do science fiction, some do historical tales or myths and legends, during a curriculum enrichment day.

Laura went back to rewrite the story with a cliff-hanger and with personalization to the characters. So when the dog is disappointed that he did not find the kitten, he must sound disappointed; a miserable woof is required. In effect facial expressions and body language need to be there in the audio.

Has Sadie used much audio so far in the classroom? Some, but usually as part of visual work; clips of films and so on. She has access to small video cameras but that can be cumbersome and would welcome the chance to use audio with its quick turnaround if equipment were there and she knew how to use it effectively. So the straightforward question remains. Would she use audio in the classroom in this way herself? Yes. Would she attempt short stories herself? As a team so those voices can be mixed up, definitely.

So finally, the graphic or poster which we suggest is shown at the same time. Not really necessary, was the conclusion, although, again for lower ability children, there could be some merit in a poster to give a visual stimulus to the creation of the character in the following literacy session and to help that child focus somewhere in the classroom as the story unfolds.

It gave Laura a credible project, thoroughly researched, and with a clear outcome. She had consulted a real client and consequently had a precise route to follow. It had also created the opportunity at least of helping a teacher tackle a tricky problem in a fresh way with a real chance of providing a solution to literacy skills in primary years. It gave a teacher the chance to perhaps use her IT skills in a new way or develop skills. It also created the opportunity to bring IT skills to the classroom via a new route because there is no reason why the more able children could not record their story when finished as an extension or differentiation exercise.

After downloading open-source edit software such as *Audacity* (see page 32), the teacher could add the original version to the child's own ending. It would not take long before the child was able to do this task themselves.

Add to that the chance to swap and share the stories across partner and cluster schools or with partner schools abroad. Comparing the story written by a child in the UK and a child in Australia or America could highlight all kinds of cultural and language nuances.

As pointed out at the start of this case study, the idea behind this has been adopted by other students I have worked with. Another girl, for example, wrote a teenage version that could be a downloadable story from a website.

This simple project involving a little girl and her missing kitten now addresses creative writing, speaking and listening, IT, teacher continuing professional development (CPD), sharing best practice and resource-building, as well as confidence-building all round and personalization. The choice of story could no doubt also nod towards healthy schools and communities and the *Every Child Matters* agenda. It could also include parents if they were to be encouraged to write contributions or take part as actors after school or as part of a club, building those bridges once again between school and community and a shared learning experience.

Above and beyond all that, it is good fun; and if there is not time for at least a little of that sometime, somewhere, then we really have collectively lost it.

# 11 John West-Burnham: Audio as a means of developing interpersonal skills

*Professor John West-Burnham*
*Teacher, writer and consultant in leadership development. He is a sought-after*
*international speaker and coordinator of the European School Leadership Project.*

## Audio is a hugely powerful vehicle

The main points featured in this case study are:

- The use of audio as a bridging tool with the community
- The use of students' multiple social-networking tools and skills
- Audio as a means of creating social capital and a learning community
- Audio to create extended learning rather than an extended school
- The students' grasp of lateral communication can be incorporated into the classroom
- Students as creators of knowledge
- The conflicts of teacher training.

This case study was based on a recorded interview.

If you look at the way young people live their lives, they are incredibly media-rich, is the opening statement from John West-Burnham.

'It's what the Dutch futures thinker, Wim Veem, calls homo-zapiens. Young people can communicate with each other in numerous ways and often simultaneously.' Those familiar with John's work will know of his long and loud endorsement of social capital.

'One of the key components of social capital and any effective community is the notion of sophisticated social networks. And the notion we are discussing through this book is the fact that young people realize that there are multiple social networks available and that we must give them the strategies to build on that.'

So what is John's definition of the phrase 'social capital'?

'Essentially it is the idea that our lives are made more effective to the extent that we build rich and sophisticated networks. Social capital is all about effective relationships and it is really building capacity in people to act and think in an interdependent way. So projects discussed in this book where students have to cooperate, work together, have to agree on how to work together, are all manifestations of social capital.'

I pointed out to John that one of the most important targets for me from the use of audio in the classroom was the possibility of providing the extended learning opportunity that could connect with the wider local community.

'Absolutely, because one of the key concepts of social capital is the notion of bonding and bridging,' he replied. 'Bonding is what most schools do; they have an identity as a community and every school in the country works hard to do that through building a sense of identity often manifested by uniform, shared values, school rituals, songs and so on.

'The trick is to be good at bonding and then to bridge out into the wider community. And schools historically are not good at this. *Every Child Matters* and the whole notion of building learning capacity does rely on schools becoming much better at bridging. And that means that they need strategies that are going to be recognizable by, and acceptable to, the community they want to bridge to.'

There is of course the clear, yet so often overlooked, option of the community giving some of its learning back to the school, which is another somewhat obvious advantage from the ability to bridge.

Although not discussed directly in this recorded conversation with John, there are a number of side issues that arise. If we take this digital learning train of thought to some sort of conclusion, does it necessarily follow that all learning must be carried out within a school, or that all the most effective learning for a given subject can be achieved within those four walls? Why the assumption that the most cost-effective delivery can only be in that school? If a student achieves more and increases their deep understanding of a subject by learning in the wider community, then surely the benefit outweighs the cost. At that point we have extended learning as an opportunity, rather than the idea of an extended school that merely offers a broader range of subjects. Extended learning meets personalization meets aspirations.

What is suggested here is that many young people already have a network to call upon – an address book on their mobile phone is a social network – and a basic grasp of some of the technology to be able to fully utilize that. They are able to share knowledge and to develop a deeper understanding of a subject by using their network and those of others. Teachers now have an opportunity to share their understanding by locking into the lateral approach already adopted by their students to create a win-win situation.

Easily said, of course, and yet the much debated digital divide argument is not only still with us but only getting worse, according to some observers. Providing hardware is not necessarily the answer to bridging the divide. Thomas Watson of IBM is, in 1943, supposed to have said, 'I think there is a world market for maybe five computers'. There are many who say that the comment could never have come directly from him, but nevertheless it is not that long ago in the grand scheme of things that people in the industry doubted the need for computers in the home.

Now the answer to everything seems to be buying some resources and then everything will be okay. Diane Lewis (see Chapter 13) argues that if a lesson is taken from a chalkboard to *PowerPoint* then all we have done is get nowhere very quickly. The resources are only part of the issue and must be complemented by leadership prepared to loosen the notion of top-down learning, to encourage new ways of amassing learning. Technology is fine if you can understand what advantages it brings and how you can use it beyond a traditional method of working. Someone needs to show you what to do with it, in other words.

As John points out, communication within employer organizations and schools tends to be top-down. In communities, communication is lateral and education has a big problem with that.

'Traditionally the teacher stands at the front as the font of knowledge, providing information in an authoritative way. But what is argued through this book is that students create knowledge and then communicate it.'

The education system is still not comfortable with that as a scenario, argues John. The system should consider partnership working with students as a more common approach than currently seen.

'We cannot say at the moment that there is a monopoly on what knowledge is and that is a huge problem for the academic community that believes it has control of knowledge. Of course we know and should accept that knowledge, in the multimedia age of the internet, is freely available to anyone.'

One of the key components of audio in the classroom remains the skill of simply using words to create an emotion and response in an audience; to motivate someone to do something they had not planned to do – for example, to buy a product, listen to a piece of music, watch a film. Add to that the skill of creating a corporate and product image to run alongside. As an example, I recounted the tasks I had previously set Year 10 BTEC students in the past, centred on radio commercials as part of Unit 5 on audio production.

I tell students to write three radio commercial scripts for a product of their choice – anything from a new dance and R'n'B album, an expensive car or a microwavable snack to one of those Ibiza-type holidays for the over 18s that parents with young children try to avoid like the plague.

The words and vocal treatment will be considerably different for the holiday than for the top-of-the range luxury car you imagine gliding effortlessly around some alpine road. The students invariably write a not very convincing script that just about covers the brief.

It is usually not very good, which is hardly surprising when we consider the range of skills required and the fact that they have probably not done anything like it before.

When read aloud, the words are monotone and ineffective, but once the tools of radio are applied, the project, in almost every instance, comes alive. They listen to their recorded voices and understand that they sound flat, uninterested and unlikely to motivate an audience. Once music, effects and careful editing are added to the newly modulated vocal track, the project becomes instantly recognizable. Every word is there for a reason.

It is now a 30-second piece of audio aimed at a specific target audience, which talks to the audience in the way they expect to be spoken to. These are very sophisticated communication skills without any reliance on visual imagery.

'And that raises for me two related issues,' says John. 'One is that you are actually building social capital by developing interpersonal skills, both in terms of communicating with an audience and in terms of a production team working together – and that is massive in terms of emotional understanding and literacy and what might be called social intelligence. Simply being aware of an audience, as in this radio commercial example, is amazing because as we all know it is difficult for adolescents to engage with humanity sometimes.

'And for me the second point is the underpinning component of any aspect of social capital in that work of this type creates a learning community, and therefore in working through a topic like this and later understanding why that commercial did or did not work, it creates an effective learning community.'

A project like these radio commercials also gives the student the opportunity to be aware of their own contributions, or lack of contributions; then they are beginning to understand how people collaborate and work together in a real workplace.

Any means of communication, which is a crucial part of social capital, is going to have the potential to reinforce student engagement. John West-Burnham also suggests that teachers are somewhat cautious about this because of their own uncertainty in terms of their own engagement with technology.

'If we look at the whole issue of personalization in learning, then we should be identifying the optimum way in which a young person is going to engage with his or her learning. And if that means multimedia approaches, and particularly audio, then that has to be seen as a significant way forward.'

John is a big fan of audio, full stop. He is not a big fan of an education system that has yet to wake up and realize that it does not have all the answers or the right to assume that it knows best. Students live the twenty-first century now and arguably are being held back in part by an educational hierarchy that stubbornly refuses to accept that the economic world has left it behind.

'We still have a model of vocational education rooted in the twentieth century and we are not looking at alternative models of what a vocation might be. Everybody pays lip service to the idea of living in an information society but does not actually realize that huge numbers of jobs in the future will be concerned primarily with different types of media and different modes of communication. And that will be real work. I think part of the problem is that we tend to see media as entertainment and not education.

'The problem is we have almost an academic snobbery and elitism about media, particularly audio; even Media Studies is seen as a marginal subject and I think that is because of the hierarchy that we have in this country based on what a proper programme of study is.

'Remember this is a generation issue too. I have been working this morning with the radio on, as background noise. Tonight, if I decide to watch some television I will search desperately for something to watch because it's all rubbish. Therefore, my mindset as regards media is that it is background noise in the car or while I'm working, or, in spite of having I don't know how many hundreds of channels, I can't find anything I want to watch. Therefore that automatically confirms my prejudice that media is either marginal or superficial.'

What then should be the role of the teacher-training centre?

'There are two conflicting imperatives here,' argues John West-Burnham. 'One is that teacher training is rooted to the performance agenda and to the national curriculum. Therefore, what's happening is that trainee teachers are essentially being brought into the culture of delivery of the national curriculum. The contradiction here is that these young people are the ones that are media savvy. A 21 year old now will be very computer literate and could use the full range, and therefore, to some extent, their experience of learning to be a teacher is often in contradiction to their own life experience.'

So, many young teachers will be experienced media practitioners in their private lives and yet not formally encouraged to join the dots in their future classroom practice.

'These young teachers are expected to lead a double life; a private life as communicators and then the artificiality of their professional life as teachers.'

A cursory look at blogs on the internet will throw up teachers confused, and sometimes openly critical, at the quality of a leadership style that pays lip service to digital practices. I suggested to John that more needs to be done to support leaders who now find themselves in decidedly unfamiliar territory.

'Then again, coffee time at headteacher conferences is mobile time as ring tones go off in all directions. And I do think more are increasingly aware of how dependent they are becoming on different types of communication and the fact that many of them are using their phones and laptops to engage with a conference, and so there is change.

'The problem is, a bit like those trainee teachers, there are conflicting imperatives here. One is the reality of people's lives and the other is the nature of the curriculum, and the two are apart.'

That aside, John West-Burnham is a serious fan of audio as just one of the tools in the teacher's digital toolkit and visualizes an exciting future. The trick, albeit somewhat simplistic, is perhaps to light the blue touch paper and stand well back. In other words, give students and teachers the resources they need, but more critically, the understanding of that technology to take learning into a convincing twentieth-first century environment.

# 12 Heat Rays 87.8 FM: The school FM radio station

All the theory about licences and transmitters and legal requirements is one thing. What teachers and students want to know is how does this work in the real world?

These are some comments from students who took part in Heat Rays 87.8 FM during the summer in 2007.

> 'I would recommend it to anyone, and the independence aspect of sorting out the features and running a show is amazing'
> **Charlotte, aged 15**

> 'Where to start? It's been an amazing week. I may have found a potential career.'
> **Gemma, aged 17**

> 'Each day was a success. It makes you more confident and if you make mistakes, you learn to overcome them.'
> **Anna aged, 15**

> 'Not only was I expected to react to my peers but also with those both younger and older than me. Also, with strangers I was expected to interview. I enjoyed Heat Rays . . . despite the early mornings!'
> **Emily, aged 16**

Restricted Service Licence (RSL) radio stations run from a school can be hugely rewarding, a significant recruitment tool and a credible example of community bridging.

Heat Rays 87.8 FM was a radio station by students for students in rural Lincolnshire. The odds were not stacked in its favour. The geography and overall lack of media choice and awareness in the area is entirely familiar to those who live in isolated rural communities. There was little heritage of radio with only one BBC local radio and one commercial station based in the county; Lincolnshire, which straddles the east coast from Yorkshire to Norfolk, is one of the largest counties in England. Heat Rays was broadcast for the first time in the early summer of 2006 from Monks' Dyke Technology College in Louth. It has its own purpose-built radio studio that, coincidentally, is also used on occasion by the local BBC station and other stations around the country.

The studio was built a few years before as a secondary local radio facility with rack-mounted CD and mini-disc players, several mic inputs and ISDN facilities fed through a professional desk. (See Chapter 7 for more on studios for schools).

So the equipment was there but the students were not, and the potential listening public had no real sense of what was to follow. Leading the project with me was Robin Webber-Jones, who at the time, was with *Chill Enterprises* in Leicester. It quickly became apparent that although some students had used the equipment before, many had not and had no idea what a programme was or how to create one. A lunchtime and after-school radio club that had run on an ad hoc basis was one thing; producing two-hour live programmes every day was quite another.

We were clear from the outset that this must be run by students for students, with adults' way away from microphones. Mixing the two would only confuse and fragment the potential audience leaving us with the possibility that there would indeed be no listeners. Robin had plenty of experience managing *Takeover Radio* in Leicester, England's first full-time station run by students for students. My experience lay in BBC radio production and I had one serious reservation from the start.

We had clearly defined our target audience as teenagers, and if they found the programming inferior or amateurish from day one, we were doomed. Peer support was critical; the target audience was critical which meant that speech and music content had to be very focused and precise. Awkward emails and texts to the station in the first couple of days would have killed the project. As it happened, my fears were totally unjustified. It worked incredibly well and there were some simple reasons for that. From day one we made it clear to all involved that this was a professional project. There was no room for casual attitudes and those not fully committed would not be welcome. We also stressed that this was about having fun and that it was most certainly possible to combine professionalism with having a great time on something that was breaking new ground.

This was the first time a school in Lincolnshire had attempted 24-hour live FM broadcasting. Monks' Dyke did have a track record here though on ambitious broadcast projects. It was the only school in England a couple of years previously to produce regular year-long programming on a weekly basis for its BBC local radio station as part of an NVQ qualification. It had also been the base for a fortnightly 30-minute local news programme produced by mature students for local cable provider *ntl*. Heat Rays was externally funded with all expenses covered so there were no last minute financial headaches or drains on school budgets.

Some funders may insist on community involvement or stipulate an age range. For example, that first summer, students aged 14 plus could take part; the second summer, there were no restrictions. However, we did work with a local hospital radio that provided specialist music programming from 6pm until 8pm. From that point, we provided an automated service and again this was crucial to the success. If your school radio stops at 6pm followed by silence, your hard-earned audience, not connected with the school, may turn that dial and go elsewhere never to return. However, if you provide a 24-hour service, it's likely they won't be bothered with retuning and will be back with your breakfast show.

Radio has been 24 hours for many years now in the UK and it is what people expect. So you may need to invest in an automatic music playout system for your studio PC. There are plenty of systems around of varying sophistication and price tags. It need not cost a fortune – a few hundred pounds – and once you have bought one, that's it. We first selected then met with our chosen students for the first summer's broadcast several months before – involve the students as early as possible. As this was to be a summer station, we gathered the students together and got them to decide on the station name, playing around with various words that they wrote on a board – sun, heat, sunshine and so on until Heat Rays FM was arrived at. They immediately had ownership of the project. Some of those students had a little experience of radio but most had never sat in front of a microphone. But they were all listeners which meant they knew what should, in theory, come out of the speaker.

We assembled programme teams from the pool of 15 students over two weekend training sessions. Some were friendship groups, others not. Experience has shown that mixing students of different ages together in one team has proved enormously beneficial, not just in terms of the project, but in the long-term school or college relationships. They benefit from different experiences of those age groups and attitudes. Once programme teams had been formed, we then sent some out into the town with a hard disk recorder. They asked local retailers and market stall holders to record a simple 'I'm Joe Bloggs from Bloggs Record Store and I listen to Heat Rays FM . . .' Around a dozen of these were put together. It is a quick and effective way of getting on-air public endorsement and helps to create that initial word of mouth publicity.

Large full-colour posters were also given to shops to display, paid for out of the funding. A good quality design on good paper always gives the right message about the quality of the service and credibility. The remaining teams were sent to quiet corners to work on programme ideas after first being reminded of the legal requirements they faced. An RSL is no different to any radio station. There are standards of behaviour to follow and that obviously means no swearing, or broadcasting songs with offensive lyrics. So they were warned to be careful of album versions of singles. There is very often a difference between the lyrics of album and radio-friendly single versions and you must be aware of that because broadcasting offensive language cannot be tolerated.

We showed them the clock method of programme planning. Draw a circle on a board and mark out in slices like a pie to show how long each programme item or song will last. Clearly each clock, or pie, will last one hour so it's simple to see at a glance how much time is left to fill. But beware at this point. People always over-estimate how long it takes to say or do something. Thirty seconds is a very long time. Try it now using your watch. You can say a great deal in that time. So students will allocate five minutes for an intro not realizing that five minutes is forever.

A couple of features, a competition, a live guest and a programme is planned. We have worked with teams of 12 year olds compiling a one-hour daily programme and it is perfectly manageable. From my own experience, finding guests willing to take part is not a problem. Students during the Heat Rays projects contacted a range of people such as the town mayor, retailers, leading local sports personalities and even the county assistant chief constable who joined the breakfast team live in the studio. If guests are asked relevant, intelligent questions and they see some gain in being involved in a positive project involving young people, they will take part. As mentioned before, critical to the success is the reaction from the student's peers. If their peer group accept it as radio they want to listen to, it can't fail.

The programme presenters must be given sufficient room to be themselves and talk in the language the audience expects to hear. If adults interfere and impose their will too clearly, in content or style, the audience will turn their backs. On school RSLs I have been involved with, we have also made sure that not only did the students record their own jingles or idents for branding purposes, but also had access to an email address and text number for the audience. The numbers of texts for 'shout outs' can climb remarkably as the days go.

Not only does this give an instant connection between student and listener, and the chance to hear their name mentioned, but it also gives a very basic indication of audience figures and reaction. One Heat Rays RSL I worked on in Louth fell on the very last week of the summer term and into the first full day of the holidays. Hundreds of students were out on school trips to attractions all over the country on two of those days, leaving the rest of us rattling around the building. Yet we still had texts running into three figures quashing the theory that only students on site were taking part and listening.

Letting a group of young students near live microphones may fill teachers with dread and fear, but the truth is, they can do it, and do it very well indeed. They will respond to the confidence shown in them and a desire to gain respect. The teachers or trainers should be there advising, supporting, mentoring and listening at all times the station is on air, but it must be a light touch. From my own rule of thumb, if a middle-aged adult likes the output, we've probably got it wrong. There is always room, as with the hospital radio example, to introduce a different programme style, in common with most radio stations, after 6pm when the TV is switched on.

Training of students at some level at least, is vitally important. They do need to know how to operate the equipment, to be able to write short script pieces and gel as a team. I have been asked to take part in RSLs with older students in other centres and refused simply because it was a free-for-all, with little or no hand on the rudder from adults, no realistic training or advice beforehand. Teachers leading RSLs should know when to stand back, but let it be known that they are there should things start to go wrong. Students also need to have absolute confidence that the adults know exactly what they are doing and talking about. A great deal of public money has been invested so it needs to be right, but the rewards for students, parents and families, the school and its wider community can be very great indeed. If schools are to adopt the ethos of community leaders in their own right, as standard bearers, then what better way than this? The memories and credibility live far longer than the individual project.

A final word on publicity. It all depends on how approachable your local press is and how busy the world is at the time. No easy answers here. The best plan is to write your own news release and email it directly to the news desk. Look at the paper concerned and write in a style that the journalist would use, with a good 'top line.' Attach a couple of photographs of students taking part (as Jpeg attachments) with a caption. Don't just take the boring head and shoulders picture which is never likely to be seen but, instead, find some way of adding value; a student doing a mock interview with a recognizable local figure; a small crowd of students all gathered around one microphone with beaming faces – anything that attracts attention and inspires the local paper to print. Make sure, of course, that the necessary parental permissions have been granted. The golden rule is: do the journalist's work for them and you are more likely to get coverage. If you just call the paper and ask for a reporter and photographer to visit, you could be in for a very long wait.

So how do we sum this up? Hard work, yes. A bit complicated the first time? Possibly. The rewards, however, as already hinted, can be enormous. You will see your students grow before your eyes, in confidence, in self-esteem, in maturity. They will form friendships not previously possible. Some will become leaders and mentors for young students by default. Their relationship with you may change for the better as you both go through a challenging experience for the first time. The real rewards though come from those students previously out of the loop – the disillusioned or disaffected who found nothing in school to call their own. Those students who sat at the back in the corner who felt that no one wanted to listen to anything they had to say. Time and again it's those students who find the key to the door they've been looking for. The sudden realization that they can communicate, that people do listen, that they already have most of the technical skills or can pick them up very quickly because it's a technological environment they are used to; that maybe they have some skills, even if it is something as simple as music awareness, from which others can benefit. It can be a liberating experience.

Of course, there is the possibility that this project opens career potentials previously not recognized because there was no other opportunity to bring that to light. I have certainly worked with students on RSLs with no experience that obviously had a tremendous natural talent. Not everyone can communicate effectively on their own with a microphone in a closed room, but then, they are not likely to know until given the opportunity.

For teachers, there is the realization that technology need not always be a substitute or perhaps an irritation, but instead a highly effective means of engaging students in a supportive, collaborative project. Technology and creativity that could be harnessed in a multitude of ways to enrich, and perhaps even transform the way the curriculum is delivered.

Finally, to close the circle, such a project defines schools and the community. The community is a stakeholder in this and it's more than recruiting volunteers or interviewees to take part. Projects such as this connect school to family to townspeople. They hold up a mirror and reflect what that community is about and bond in an instantaneous way. The stories and features covered celebrate what that community thinks about, cares about, believes in, argues and laughs about. If education is a community responsibility, then here it is.

# 13 Diane Lewis: Audio by email from the UK to the USA

*Diane Lewis*
*Director of Instructional Technology, Seminole County Public Schools, Florida*

## Atlantic crossings

The main points featured in this case study are:

- Transferring a lesson across to *PowerPoint* is not the best use of technology
- Student reflections on the use of technology in the twenty-first century classroom
- An example of transatlantic cooperation
- The importance of authentic audiences for student work
- Looking beyond the tools of audio and concentrating on the outcomes.

Diane Lewis is an authority on the use of technology in classrooms, is very enthusiastic and raises some interesting issues.

On Diane's website, she states clearly that if we continue to use technology merely as a slightly different way of doing what we have always done, then we can hardly expect students to benefit from deep learning or learn more efficiently. If the use of technology amounts to transferring a lesson onto a *PowerPoint* presentation, then perhaps this is not using what is out there to the best advantage.

The option of sending audio across the Atlantic in seconds from one school to another was science fiction until comparatively recently in the big scheme of things. When we tried such a project in late 2007 between the UK and Florida, it nevertheless still generated considerable excitement amongst students taking part. Nothing perhaps compared to December 12, 1901 at 12.30 when three faint clicks were heard in Signal Hill, Newfoundland.

Gugliemo Marconi had sent three dots of Morse code – the letter S. The weak signal in Canada was result of a major scientific breakthrough by Marconi using a makeshift wireless station on a cliff at Poldhu in Cornwall, England.

Marconi's efforts were deeply appreciated although not directly credited at the end of his Morse project. His massive £50,000 gamble in 1901 had paid off, but, with classic reserve, the British press and establishment were gloriously unimpressed while the Canadians gave Marconi £16,000 towards the cost of a permanent wireless station.

The original building in Cornwall was demolished in 1934; however, a new permanent building now sits there, not as a replica, but more to catch the spirit of the time. An amateur radio group, GB2GM, is still there. Whether, as a result, this lonely, desolate place in the cliff-top field at the edge of the Lizard Peninsula is the birthplace of radio, internet and mobile phone technologies, as enthusiasts suggest, is a matter for debate. But the significance is not an issue. That broadcast over 1,700 miles of ocean at the beginning of the twentieth century now makes routine projects for schools and colleges at the beginning of the twenty-first century a reality.

Diane got in touch at the start of the academic year in 2007 to ask whether we would be prepared to take part in a small audio project. She had recently taken responsibility for technology across dozens of schools in Seminole County in Florida.

We should get our bearings first. Seminole County markets itself as 'the other side' of Orlando. Fewer crowds, less traffic and still with the usual Florida trappings that so appeal to UK visitors in particular: If you look at a map, Universal Studios is just over there, to the left. So this is a fast-paced location with high levels of media attention and all round communication and technology bombardment. The UK students were all from very quiet rural locations with little in the way of media outlets or opportunities to soak up technology and what it can offer.

Diane was particularly interested to know how students in the UK felt technology should be used to help their learning. She was also interested in any examples of how it had helped. Four students were assembled, two 14-year-old boys, two 14-year-old girls, all Year 10.

The idea was simple enough, record the students' views, get that down to five minutes and get it across to the States. We had five working days to fit this in to odd bits of spare time. A list of around five questions were prepared by Diane and emailed across. We got the students together and pressed record. What happened of course was twenty minutes of something or other with occasional nods to the questions. Added to that was a sprinkling of 14-year-old English language. 'Defo,' said one girl repeatedly when asked a question. 'Yeah, defo.'

This, you will be relieved to know, was nothing to do with any hearing impediment but a short form of 'definitely '.Text-speak as well as text writing is here to stay. When we played the piece back we had to point this out to the team and raise the possibility that the average Floridian teenager may not be up to speed. They will naturally have their own teenage-speak but the meanings may not translate too well.

It seems a minor point, but we were trying to put across some serious suggestions in a short space of time and it was important that this piece was presented in such a way that everyone understood the answers without hidden meanings. 'Defo' was ditched. That still left us with a stream of answers that could never be boiled down from twenty minutes. But this was a lunchtime rehearsal. We knew the students would be nervous and unsure even though they had seen the questions in advance. That was why I had suggested the Thursday afternoon session. In the back of my mind was the fact that this audio had to be in America by the following Wednesday at the latest. Monday was the allocated lunchtime recording for real. That gave the students time to digest how the recording had gone and think again about their shortened and considerably more focused answers.

The UK students considered the use of *wikis* and of blogs to make points and write thoughts down. They considered the use of flash pens or MP3 players as standard kit to move work around from school to home.

One girl recounted her experience of taking part in a school RSL FM radio station the previous summer. She made a particular point about how the real radio audience had a marked effect on her confidence. When she or any of her programme team asked for text messages or music requests, the texts duly followed. She remarked on the sheer excitement of that positive, instantaneous response to her work from complete strangers. Of course, a radio programme is a somewhat extreme example of how to use technology as Diane points out: 'The radio show isn't the answer for every classroom and every student, but finding ways to incorporate authentic audiences and voice works whether it's a radio show, a podcast, a movie or digital story, a wiki, blog or website featuring student writing.'

Monday came and that time to rethink certainly paid off with an almost perfect recording that lasted around eight minutes which was easy enough to cut down to five.

Tuesday evening was edit time and I recorded a brief link at the end to bookend the piece so it had a definite start and finish. It was emailed that night and duly arrived in Florida moments later, in fact late morning in Florida thanks to the five-hour difference, way ahead of the Wednesday deadline.

The excitement, certainly from the UK end, was palpable. It is such a simple idea, so easy to do and yet we imagine that all teenagers are now so used to technology that they treat every such experience as entirely normal. The thought that they could talk to students thousands of miles away within minutes and that their views were taken seriously and had value, was a real lift to their spirits.

Remember, that exchange could be a piece of creative writing, an audio postcard or even a piece of music. It could be stand-alone or require completion at the other end. The net result was that Diane wanted to get more projects off the ground as soon as practically possible. So was it all a success? Defo.

In Florida, there was equal enthusiasm. As Diane pointed out some months later: 'I was so impressed by the 'underlying' messages that the kids shared. The importance of authentic audience; the meaningfulness of having your message heard in the community, not just the classroom or the school; the need for information to be digital, portable and accessible 24/7. These ideas underscored much of what the kids talked about.

'It was the main point I made when our visioning team listened to your students, and they felt that listening with those points in mind made a difference – to listen beyond the words they use and get to the meaning. Getting to these meanings helps us to avoid focusing on a specific tool and focus on the outcomes that we want, using a variety of tools that will change over time.'

## Where are the schools for international projects?

Basically there are tens of thousands of schools out there looking for partners right now. There will be countless websites, many hosted locally in individual countries, that will offer help. This following is by no means a definitive list, but simply a few possible suggestions that barely scratch the surface:

- Personally, I have found the British Council to be very helpful in the past when looking for partner schools or colleges. A school can register its details, what its interests are and wait for others to connect in the way of a social networking opportunity. The British Council Learning site has around 10,000 schools waiting and actively looking for partners for all manner of reasons, some of course, looking for student exchanges. I received regular emails from schools from as far as India and Africa that had seen my details on the Council's website and wanted to get in touch offering collaboration on various projects.

- The European Commission's Lifelong Learning Programme has eTwinning. At the time of writing there were 31,000 schools across Europe on the site register. There is a real depth of information with practical project suggestions and information on what schools are doing across Europe and the local teaching and education standards of that country. Although it does appear that it is not updated that frequently.

- Japan 21 provides a free schools connection service between the UK and Japan, working closely with the British Council in Tokyo. As well as the initial contact there is back-up and advice available. However, they do stress that any contact should be viewed as a long-term commitment and it may not be possible to find a Japanese school willing to take part in a short-term one-off project. It may be possible to apply to the British Council for funding for a joint curriculum project with a Japanese school but, of course, funding streams come.

    There is also the e-link project and the aim was to bring Japanese and UK students closer together and give students in Japan a direct look at life in the UK as it is now. It was also created to break down stereotypical views, build lasting partnerships and motivate students to learn English. Grants have been available to set up such projects in the past; again it is worth asking to see if that still applies.

- Link Community Development works with children across Africa. The Link Schools Programme facilitates mutually beneficial partnerships between over 700 schools in Ireland, the UK, Ghana, Uganda, South Africa and Malawi.
- Connecting Classrooms provides cluster groups of three schools with the chance to partner schools from two different countries in sub-Saharan Africa with one from the UK. Schools apply as groups of three and are invited to a partnership seminar. Those schools are then in theory matched with three schools from one African country and three from a second. At time of writing there were grants of up to £15,000 available, £5,000 per cluster for up to three years. The programme involves Botswana, Cameroon, Eritrea, Ethiopia, Ghana, Kenya, Lesotho, Mauritius, Malawi, Mozambique, Namibia, Nigeria, South Africa, Senegal, Sierra Leone, Sudan, Tanzania, Uganda, Zambia, Zimbabwe and the four countries of the UK.

  Possible projects could include, for example, literacy and language learning. This could include story-telling, cultural heritage and the development of literary traditions. Drama might include a joint creation of a play or dramatic event with each cluster contributing to a partnership production. The environment is a significant topic for science. This could include comparing weather and the ways different cultures perceive and are prepared or able to tackle climate change. A citizenship project gives an opportunity to focus on global citizenship looking at intercultural understanding or healthy eating, stereotypes or entrepreneurial activities; all cross-curricular and all suitable for audio outcomes.
- DFID Global School Partnerships connects schools in the UK and schools in Africa, Asia, Latin America and the Caribbean. The Department for International Development (DFID) has funded the DFID Global School Partnerships (DGSP) programme since 2003. At time of writing the delivery contract was about to expire and up for tender, however, the following contract awarded to the successful delivery consortium will run until at least 2010.

What about the compatibility of schools to the UK and their education systems? The briefest of research will throw up some interesting facts. ICT in the Netherlands, for example, is a core curriculum component along with internationalization, so this would appear to be knocking at an open door as far as partnerships are concerned. English language is mandatory until the final year exam so teachers and students have little difficulty communicating.

ICT is widely used across education and is therefore the rule rather than exception with high levels of computer access. Dutch schools are interested in projects involving the exchange of lifestyles and this is often via web blogs and forums. However, as we have discovered with Diane Lewis, exchanging pre-recorded audio emails or blogs is incredibly simple. English is the dominant language. Twenty per cent of schools taking part in eTwinning projects in 2007 were from the primary sector and they were keen to develop links with special needs education.

Compare this with Slovakia which is equally keen on partnership collaborations. Keen it may be, but the resources it has are not in the same quantity as other European countries. However, all schools are internet connected. Times are changing but the ethos has been on far more formal memory-based learning with less opportunity for creativity.

The government is aware of the need for its young people to be able to compete in a global economy and recognized that with the document *Policy of Informatisation of Society in the Slovak Republic* which was adopted in Resolution No. 43 on January 21, 2004. It is safe to say that there will be a warm welcome for UK schools.

# 14 The Leicester Experience: Audio by young people, for young people

*Robin Webber-Jones*
*Currently the Curriculum Manager for Media at South Leicestershire College and is a Director of the creative writing and radio production not-for-profit company,* Crystal Clear Creators, *of which he was a founder member. Previously he was the Trust Manager of Takeover Radio Children's Media Trust (September 2003–September 2005) and then moved on to be the Training and Development Director of* Chill Enterprises Limited, *a not-for-profit social enterprise that he helped set up to support young people into the creative industries.*

The main points featured in this case study are:

- Robin Webber-Jones, a personal perspective
- Woodstock Primary School
- Takeover Radio
- Kimberly's story
- Scheme of work and lesson plan.

Robin has compiled the following case study from projects he has worked on or been associated with.

More than 18 per cent of the British population is under the age of 15, yet they do not have a radio station to call their own – apart from in one part of the Midlands. There are, and have been, various stations for young people (some of them even by young people) but all but one has survived. Yet it has been proved, by a range of people using a range of methods, that engaging young people in the recording of audio can have a positive effect on their lives. In the *Radio in School's Pilot Programme* by the Radio Academy, BBC, and Sheffield Hallam University in 2001, it was noted that once 'radio' was introduced there was a rise in attainment within students. This raise may have been a result of increased self-esteem and, or because of the collaborative skills, but results rose across the ability spectrum.

In recent times in education there has been much discussion about how the attainment and intrinsic motivation of learners can be increased in order to ensure that young people remain in education and employment. Nationally, it is recognized that males appear to be most disadvantaged. In the context of many of our inner cities it is mainly the white working-class groups that suffer most. For example, the profile of boys at all key stages in the UK in July 2001 suggests that over two years, especially at National Curriculum level 5, females achieve far higher than males academically; in some cases up to 16.8 per cent higher, and in most averaging approximately 8 per cent. The only exceptions are maths at levels 4 and 5, and science at level 6.

A reason often cited for poor attainment is behaviour. Therefore, the notion of the research is to find additional activities that can be used in the context of teaching radio which can be used to 'train the brain'.

One extremely important purpose of emotions from an evolutionary perspective is to help us decide what to remember and what to forget. The brain develops these memories through the way it is structured. A new-born child is not aware of its position as an individual, but as we get older we feel a sense of belonging to the environment around us and our relationships to other groups such as family and friends. What becomes of most significance is a sense of belonging; those that feel a connection of belonging thrive. If an individual does not feel connected to society, or the institutions within it, then he or she will try to get noticed by misbehaving, playing up, and annoying others.

In a recent project with a group of learners, I focused on using audio to allow the young people who were all 16 and under to connect with the world around them by creating a range of features. They were able to record and re-record their ideas. They were able to choose subjects particular to them, and work in small groups to script ideas.

From the outset, it is worth considering that just because audio is the medium, any art form or project could be used to encourage the learners. Over the course of an academic year, work was carried out with a group of hesitant learners to get them to explore. The rituals of turning up on time and drafting and re-drafting ideas are some of the key reasons why they react aggressively to the world around them; they have never previously been encouraged to engage with such activity. This is the key thing to draw from the activities. Activities that encouraged learners to review the patterns within the brain can help them to succeed so that positive brain patterns emerge. However, a more longitudinal study will need to be undertaken to assess if these changes would lead to developing intrinsic motivation. Of note is that these learners had me for an entire day. It meant that the learners could bond with me at the earliest possible opportunity.

One of the central areas of focus was the fact that the group spent much time and energy focusing on humiliating each other, especially in the early stages of the observations, and this actually hindered the teaching of radio. While it can be argued that this is a basic biological process, it does mean that the group did not have a natural propensity to work together. A series of sub-groups formed, which allowed students to help each other, but it meant that natural flaws were accentuated. Learners needed a lot of input to get on with the work, and there was an apparent inability to think about the challenge themselves. Due to the high levels of energy and aggressive behaviour, Socratic versions of teaching were also used while doing the exercises. This meant walking around with them to release excess energy. This can often be difficult to do when teaching radio as the practical elements are based in a studio. However, discussion during the exercises meant that this was easy to achieve. The negative behaviour was reversed after the six weeks of observation, and after undertaking the exercises. This demonstrated that they started to understand how their behaviour was influencing others.

One of the most significant things I noted in classroom observations across the six weeks is that I think differently to my students and, therefore, react differently to them. They deal with anger in the only way they know how, in the way that their brain patterns have emerged over the years.

The first thing to note is that the teacher was motivated by radio, whereas the student often showed resistance to new ideas. Again, this is a conditioned behaviour, and through the study it has become apparent that the teacher should focus on reminding learners of the distance they have travelled. This means that they may be able to consider their improvements and find greater connectivity with the tasks. The process of putting a broadcast together was used to infuse good citizenship in the classroom. This involved using the activities to create a sense of respect, towards the teacher, towards each other and towards their work. This meant controlling volume levels and ensuring all learners take responsibility for their actions.

Of great significance was that radio could be used as a means of encouraging students to relate to each other. Through the discussions it became increasingly obvious that the learners had never had any previous lessons or experience in how to relate to each other. Furthermore, it became apparent that there were other co-educational factors affecting their learning, such as the role that the family was playing in their development. One learner stated that the exercises were a hugely significant factor in improving his overall behaviour; he said that he began to recognize when he got angry. The act of having a challenge in producing a radio programme each week, with the same routine to the day, was providing security, and once this had been achieved learners were more willing to engage in learning activities with their peers. After understanding how brain patterns emerge, they were more willing to accept a weekly routine. One learner commented that they were developing a sense of trust. This trust was not just with myself as their tutor, but also with their peers. This is something that develops when people go through various rites of passage. Being able to complete the NOCN (National Open College Network) units, demonstrating the core skills, was, for these learners with no qualifications, a rite of passage; suddenly, there was a sense of acceptance. Due to the immaturity of these learners they are going through rites of passage at a much later age. The radio as a project and the structure of the day created a form of orderliness, which many educationalists have, through observation, noted as a central ingredient to learning.

The quality of the radio broadcasts was never of issue to the learners. It was the quality of work that mattered. Much of the learners' time in earlier education had been spent in competition with their peers. This had extended in this class as learners were in competition for attention and resources. It appears that since 2000 there has been a wide range of material published about the nature of which the brain works, backed up by a wide variety of anger management tools. However, what has not been considered previously is the nature of the qualification that may best suite this type of learner, and how the behaviour support and brain pattern changing exercises need to be embedded into the mainstream.

Here lies the very essence of the problem; intrinsic motivation is something that takes time to build; students do not necessarily automatically feel ready to take on learning. Moreover, each week it was noted that there was some regression in the learners. This was because they were not getting the level of support they needed in areas such as their home life. This is central to reversing negative behaviour patterns.

Getting going can often be seen as the most complex and time-consuming process when it comes to using audio as a tool for teaching and learning. Often schools will have equipment even if just a basic dictaphone, but they may not know how to tie that into delivery of the curriculum. Given the constraints and pressures on teachers it is easy to see why. Therefore, highlighted below are several simple exercises that can be undertaken to 'get going', and extend the work already being undertaken in the classroom.

> Divide the class (or even half the class) into four groups. Groups will rotate between producing a radio show, producing a feature, recording a radio drama, and doing some music. Music will include composition, performance, sampling sequencing and audio technologies.
>
> Start off by assigning each person in the group a role. For example, someone may be the manager, someone might be head of stories and someone might be head of news and so on. Get the group to draw a circle on a piece of paper, and divide it up, like a pie chart, to highlight who is doing what – for example, each person, depending on their role, can gather the content for that piece of the show they are doing. ⇨

> This will get everyone to explore using the technologies for broadcast, edit and recording. Most importantly, it will start to get young people thinking about writing for an audience.

## INSET with teachers, especially English and IT

We will look at how radio can be used within the curriculum, perhaps to achieve some of the following:

### Radio: curriculum links

**Keystage 3**

- Citizenship (1f): the work of voluntary groups (1h), the importance of the media (3a – c); participate in the creation of a school radio station or the making of an assembly for broadcast.
- English/Media (En 1–3): create a radio magazine programme from planning stage to review. Include interviews, jingles, and news bulletins adapted for younger listeners; conduct a play or dramatized story.

**Keystage 2**

- English: literacy hour Year 5 Term 1 – experience instructional texts, develop recounal of events; develop play scripts; create for performance to audience.
- English: literacy hour Year 5 Term 2 – look at traditional stories, myths and legends; emulate these in writing for performance; non-chronological reports, explanations of events; read these to an audience.
- English: literacy hour Year 5 Term 3 – poetry, novels and stories from a variety of cultures; look at and develop choral and performance poetry; persuasive writing; put across or argue a point of view; achieve by creating commentaries on a theme and presenting to others.

In the National Framework for teaching English, there are many hard outcomes for which radio can be used as a tool. These can be found at The Standards website (www.standards. dfes.gov.uk) and include some of the following examples.

### Speaking

1 Reflect on the development of their abilities as speakers in a range of different contexts and identify areas for improvement
2 Use Standard English to explain, explore or justify an idea
3 Develop interview techniques which include planning a series of linked questions, helping the respondent to give useful answers, responding to and extending the responses

## Listening

4 Reflect on and evaluate their own skills, strategies and successes as listeners in a variety of contexts

5 Compare different points of view that have been expressed, identifying and evaluating differences and similarities

6 Analyse bias, e.g. through the use of deliberate ambiguity, omission, abuse of evidence

7 Identify the underlying themes, implications and issues raised by a talk, reading or programme

## Group discussion and interaction

8 Review the contributions they have made to recent discussions, recognizing their strengths and identifying areas for development

9 Discuss and evaluate conflicting evidence to arrive at a considered viewpoint

10 Contribute to the organization of group activity in ways that help to structure plans, solve problems and evaluate alternatives

## Drama

11 Recognize, evaluate and extend the skills and techniques they have developed through drama

12 Use a range of drama techniques, including work in role, to explore issues, ideas and meanings, e.g. by playing out hypotheses, by changing perspectives

13 Develop and compare different interpretations of scenes or plays by Shakespeare or other dramatists

14 Convey action, character, atmosphere and tension when scripting and performing plays

15 Write critical evaluations of performances they have seen or in which they have participated, identifying the contributions of the writer, director and actors.

# Woodstock Primary School, Leicester

The Y is part of the Leicester YMCA. It is a community arts venue, housing a theatre, bar, dance studio and workshop rooms, which runs its own multi-arts programme, as well as working in partnership with other organizations to run artistic activity. The Y is a partner in Leicester's Creative Partnerships scheme. This is a DfES (Department for Children, Schools and Families) and DCMS (Department for Culture, Media and Sport) funded programme which is managed by the Arts Council England (ACE). *Creative Partnerships* work with schools and young people in the most deprived communities in England, linking them with creative practitioners and organizations to improve young people's achievements and aspirations and develop schools' approach to culture and creativity.

The Y is working with Woodstock Primary School, a primary school in one of the most deprived areas of Leicester. It also has a significant number of ESOL children who have a high turnover rate, thus gaining no additional support. One of the artistic activities they are doing with them is a radio and recording project. It is a classic example of how a school can get started, and of how other organizations, without a background in audio production, can get involved in producing audio.

Initially, Woodstock Primary School got additional funding from the DfES to develop a 'space for sports and arts'. This meant some upgrades to the gym, and sound-proofing of two small rooms, and putting basic audio equipment (CD player, mixer, tape player, some mics) in one of the rooms to create a mini recording studio. However, the equipment laid dormant and unused as there had been no input into staff training. The school decided that it wanted to develop the use of audio to improve communication as the school is split-site. Furthermore, the school has changed its curriculum to be topic-based rather than subject-based. The school has been keen to pursue any activity to ensure that the children remain engaged in education so that they do not continually feel pressured.

The Y paired up with some audio specialists, who initially offered training to a group of teachers, and to some Year 3 and 4 pupils. Furthermore, some money was used to invest in equipment, which would aid any broadcast. This included an open source (i.e. free) computer automation system which would allow the children to develop a library of music. It also included some advanced editing programmes. Once the equipment was in place the children worked in classes to develop hour-long programmes. The topics in the programmes were based on evaluating and summating work conducted in class. For example, the children had worked with a fashion designer to come up with designs for bags; they then used the radio recordings as a way of developing and evaluating the work they had undertaken. The class was divided into groups to write and read individual elements. The sub-groups then worked together to develop things such as jingles, playlists and links.

There is a genuine belief that the use of audio in the classroom has worked. The pupils have been enthusiastic, as have many of the teachers, but in the present climate, it has given an added pressure to change the way of thinking. The climate also means that it will take time to get it into whole school practice. There has been some suggestion to make it extra-curricular. However, it has been noted, through children regularly commenting 'it's not work', that it is a very useful tool for delivering literacy. Furthermore, some commented how it is a useful tool for revision, once a group get to the end of a topic.

Instead of going back through a quantity of notes, information can be written, read, spoken, and listened to, and stored to re-access aurally.

Initially, despite the fact that the school had some equipment, there was a significant lack of knowledge within staff. Therefore, a specialist in the field was hired for three days. The long-term plan is to develop an in-house training scheme for pupils and teachers, so that each class will use it for each topic. As part of the creative partnerships programme, some of the students have been designated as 'young consultants' so that they work with their fellows pupils to decide where to take some of the creative work going on; they will use reporter packs and audio equipment to conduct these interviews.

In conclusion, while the project at Woodstock is in its early days, many opportunities are opening up.

# Takeover Radio, Leicester

Takeover Radio Children's Media Trust is a registered charity that has been running Takeover Radio on 103.2 FM from the centre of Leicester since 2002. The station was one of the pilot stations used to test the viability of community radio in the UK. Since then it has gone on to gain a full-time community licence. The station was put together to allow under-18s to broadcast to under-18s. The station aims to create an interesting experience for participants, and exciting credible radio for its audience, which now stands in excess of 50,000 across the city.

Most significantly, the radio station was the first full-time FM radio in the world where young people make shows for young people. Furthermore, as many counterpart radio stations broadcasting on digital radio have folded due to financial shortage, Takeover Radio has kept running.

Graham Coley is chair of the charity and has been a central figure in the development of the radio station. With the information above in mind, in order to consider how to develop the use of audio with young people, it makes sense to indulge in his knowledge of how to set such a project up.

## Why did you set the project up?

Giving confidence is useful and important. The project gives people the ability to speak out loud, and express opinions in the correct manner. When developing audio there are lots of things that people can work on, from researching and writing items to exploring additional sound effects and structure that can be added to strengthen arguments.

The starting point for creating audio is always an idea; a creative spark which is often the most difficult thing to get. Anyone can be taught how equipment operates or the functions within editing software. However, it is difficult to teach people how to be 'creative'. Technical knowledge is of course needed, but to an extent it can be kept to a minimum. The best way of learning is to try, but controls on any recording pack are the same as any control on a DVD or CD player at home, so it is not that difficult to get the basics. Moreover, editing software is like any other software.

The most important thing is how to structure an idea; how to use the research and equipment to get the desired result. Self-motivation can be one of the key elements to get results. Being able to play with research and equipment, to make mistakes and learn from them, is central to creating high-quality audio.

Once a good idea is in place, researched and recorded, it makes sense to share the work created with an audience; otherwise there is little point in undertaking the task of recording. The easiest way to broadcast is to plug a speaker into the back of the equipment and broadcast directly that way. Another way is over the web. This can be a preferable way, as it gets the work out to the wider world. This method of 'podcasting' was actually how Takeover Radio started before running its first full time licence. The digital radio platform is very expensive to broadcast on, as is broadcasting over the airwaves on AM or FM. On AM schools can apply for a 1-watt free radiating licence.

While these licences are meant to be site specific, they often have a much wider range, depending in the atmospherics. While the broadcast can be cheap, it does require some technical expertise when setting up, so people will need to consult with professional organizations.

The other way is to apply for a short-term FM (Restricted Service Licence). However, the application process is costly. Furthermore, the performing rights fees can be high when broadcasting to the general public which would include a school. The costs for hard wire broadcasting can often be covered in a school's standard PRS (Performing Rights Society) fees. Web broadcasting fees currently sit at £100 a year.

The most difficult thing in the development of Takeover has been money; as an independent charity that receives no regular funding from any source, it can be difficult to be constantly producing material. The easiest thing has been getting young people involved. As it is a thing that young people love to do, there has never been a struggle to get people involved. Schools' involvement has been limited, and the Takeover team hypothesis, that given the workload teachers are under, means that they struggle to access any other resource. However, if schools came forward with content or a desire to be trained, then they can be accommodated.

There is a team approach to quality assurance. The ethos of the station is as much to do with giving opportunities to young people of all abilities as creating a credible platform that young people will access and listen to. Therefore, not all errors cause mass panic. Quality is monitored by listening, and everyone gets to contribute in expressing an opinion of quality. Often this can be judged by listener reaction; if listeners like what they hear, they will text and email.

Training is another way in which one can tell if quality shows are produced. If the training offered to members is of quality and reflects how to put quality programming together, then it will create quality shows.

# Kimberly's story

Kimberly Alderson is from New Parks in Leicester. This is an area that is defined as deprived. Indeed, more than 50 per cent of the population does not have a qualification, and while employment is low, those that are employed tend to travel less than six miles to work.

*Where do you live? What is it like? Do you like school? What do you want to do in your wildest dreams?*

'I live in New Parks. The area is not all that good because of the gangs of youths. I liked school nearer to the end as we got better teachers that were willing to help us get our GCSEs. I would like to become a nanny and work all over the world.'

*What attracted you in getting involved in radio?*

'I heard the broadcasts for the first time in August 2006 and I thought to myself "I wouldn't mind doing that."'

*What have you done on the radio project?*

'In this radio project I was one of the radio managers where I had to help out organize the radio station and the timetable.'

*What has been the most difficult thing you have had to do as part of the project?*

'The hardest part of the project was when the main radio manager went away to do another radio station in Lincoln and someone else came in for the week.'

*How has being involved in radio/audio made you feel?*

'It has made me feel more confident in talking.'

*How has it changed your ambitions?*

'It hasn't really changed my ambitions as the radio was just an interest.'

*How has it helped you educationally?*

'I wouldn't say it helped me educationally as I had already finished school.'

*What do you think that the radio project has done for the local area?*

'The radio has interested some of the people in my local area and may show them not everyone in the area is bad as that is the point of view that most of the local people have on teenagers in the area.'

*What other skills have you gained?*

'I would say I have gained more confidence and communication skills. Also time keeping which comes in good use when you start working or when you go into further education.'

# A sample scheme of work

| Session | Activity | Tutor Activity | Learner Activity | Aims | Assessment |
|---|---|---|---|---|---|
| 1 | Warm up and introduction to anthology/setting contract | Lead a range of amusing challenges | Hopes/fears/expectations | Initial assessment on learners | Not formal |
| 2 | Introduction to first story/record and edit | Teach basics of recording/mic technique | Using anthology | Introduction to the principals of sound | Work in groups to produce a recording |
| 3 | Show planning/recording | Teach how a show works | Record show | Introduction to the notion of what radio is | Record a show |
| 4 | Additional linkages with poems, recorded and edited for 2 different audiences | Use anthology to start to draw connections and an awareness of audience | Use anthology to look at how poems link | To understand audience and using audio for English | Set the audience. Listening to 2 different types of radio station |
| 5 | Turning poems into music | Teaching Acid | Using Acid for music creation | Introduction to sampling | Completed track |
| 6 | Performing poetry | Look at different performance styles | Mini performances | Looking at the staging of words | Work towards mini performances |
| 7 | Performing poetry | Continue | Continue | As above | Mini performances |
| 8 | Station planning | Look at the elements that make a radio station | Plan and execute those elements | Putting together a complete radio station | Completed playlist/schedule and present |
| 9 | Story recording/writing | Look at formula for writing | Write and record story | Using skills gained to create an original piece | Written and recorded story |
| 10 | Story recording/writing | Continue | Continue | As above | As above |
| 11 | Story as theatre | Take story for radio and turn into stage production | Rehearse | Introduction to the principle of theatre | Introduction to theatre/spontaneity |
| 12 | Story as theatre | Continue | Continue | As above | As above |
| 13 | Musical theatre | History/form and structure of musical theatre | Look at different styles/types of performance | Look at the form of musical theatre and its use for storytelling | Techniques of musical theatre |
| 14 | Musical theatre | Continue | Continue | Perform musical theatre | Mini performance |
| 15 | TRIP | | | | |
| 16 | Collate interviews | Lead recording and editing techniques | Record and edit interviews for station | To get ready for broadcast | Record and edit 3 interviews |
| 17 | Collate interviews | Lead recording and editing techniques | Record and edit interviews for station | Ensure all is ready for broadcast | As above |
| 18 | BROADCAST | BROADCAST | BROADCAST | BROADCAST | BROADCAST |
| 19 | BROADCAST | BROADCAST | BROADCAST | BROADCAST | BROADCAST |
| 20 | Evaluation of broadcast | Lead evaluation | Complete evaluation forms | Ensure that mistakes are learnt from | Completed evaluation forms |

# 15 Mike Kinnaird: Using sound to capture the story

## Let the sounds tell the story

The main points featured in this case study are:

- The search for a distinctive personal sound
- The recording of wildtrack and actuality
- How to 'see' pictures using audio to engage an audience
- When to record in a quiet room and when to search for descriptive sounds
- Recording business studies in the High Street.

This is my own case study so please just bear with me on this. There is a point to this story.

As a young broadcast journalist with his first radio production job at the BBC, I found myself just one of hundreds of similar journalists all with vastly different skills and abilities. Some were great political animals, others interested in sport. The majority had a passion bordering on obsession for hard news. Unfortunately, a very large number did have at least one thing in common. They sounded the same. They were good writers, good journalists, good at winkling out a story from a list of reluctant interviewees, but they sounded pretty much the same. What we used to call 'clip-link packages'. The reporter reads a short script, a brief clip from the guest, another reporter link and so on. Usually a 'dry' sound was favoured, in other words, very little audio atmosphere but clean, well-recorded vocals. For whatever reason, and I cannot honestly say what it is, I wanted to sound distinctive, different in some way, produce audio that would be remembered after the three minutes had ended.

So I found myself dispatched to a seaside resort to cover the demolition of a large, imposing and very grand red brick hotel. It was to make way for a small shopping mall in the name of progress. This hotel was one of the great, towering solid hotels that punctuated the east coast line in the heyday of the railways when thousands flocked to the coast for a day away from East Midlands city grime.

I then had to record a breakfast-show piece about the demolition of this hotel. I was new to the game, no contacts, and little experience and stood with mounting gloom as numerous men set about their task with relish sending bricks and window frames flying.

This then is one of those moments when the clouds part, the sun shines and luck stares down from above. On this late winter's morning I began a conversation with another demolition onlooker who purely by chance happened to be the last manager of the hotel. He, somewhat miserably, began recounting stories of his daughter's wedding that had been held in a marquee on the lawn, now a car park to a selection of threatening machinery. Not only did he agree to be interviewed but offered to take me inside for a final look around. Risk assessments, you will have gathered, were not a high priority at the time, in fact were never discussed in those days. So with nothing more than an ill-fitting hard hat and my trusty *Uher* reel-to-reel tape recorder complete with *AKG* mic and foam wind shield, it was into the hotel.

After a few more anecdotes, we began the recording. The noise was incredible, as anyone who has stood inside a hotel that is being demolished will testify. These railway hotels were monuments to engineering and pride, and built like nuclear bunkers. Bricks rained down, wood split and cracked, and glass shattered. And in the middle of all this, I was recording and attempting a conversation, catching the emotion of this man's memories literally falling around him. Except that was all but impossible. We tried the daughter's wedding marquee story about three times and gave up as yet another shower of rubble drowned out all thoughts never mind words. The extent of my interview as recorded amounted to little more than, 'I'm sorry, can you say that again . . . ?'

Back to the studio to edit the tape and it was obviously that you could barely hear a word above what sounded like a series of explosions in a war zone. With a heavy heart I sent the audio over a landline back to base, chalking this as yet another failure in what would surely be a brief career in radio.

The following morning, after the breakfast show and back in my district office, the internal phone rang. I recognised the programme organizer's voice and waited for instructions on where to collect my P45. To my amazement he was ecstatic; beside himself with praise. On and on it went – what a brilliant piece it was, so emotional, real sense of involvement. I did manage to point out in a lull that you could barely hear a sentence. That's not the point, he replied. You were sent out to cover a grand hotel being demolished and what I heard was a grand hotel being demolished. The fact we could hardly hear the man's stories only added to the sadness of the occasion, he said. I could 'see' this building and the end of an era coming to a close.

So this is the point I am making. For me, this was a defining moment in my career. I knew now what it was that was missing in so much audio that I had listened to from others and that was the sound of something taking place. Sound is what makes great audio; words are not enough. Words can tell of a situation but it is sound that involves us in the same way that video engages the television news audience.

Creating audio for a classroom situation should be no different. If a teacher is simply going to record their voice and play it back then what exactly has been achieved?

I had learned an invaluable lesson that stayed with me throughout my career. The creative use of sound engages an audience. It makes them feel part of what you are saying. They can relate to it in many ways by recalling memories and images of their own to add to your piece. They get a sense of being there and that they are no longer an outsider but part of what is taking place. My daily mantra became 'what will it sound like?' Before I left the building, before I met the guest, before I recorded a single word, I ran the story through in my head working out what might it sound like coming out of a speaker. That way, when I arrived at a location, I could record some pieces to fit the plan in my head, hopefully turning a potentially dry 'clip-link' piece into something a little more interesting and engaging. Of course I always balanced that with what I saw and heard when I arrived. Where there any other sounds not previously accounted for that I could use to illustrate what I wanted to say?

There are plenty of stories like these in the bank of many broadcast journalists to draw upon. There I was, sat in the passenger seat of a rally car – except of course there was no seat – as it hurtled off at mind-altering speeds up a racetrack straight in order to publicize a forthcoming event. You want sound, then try that for size – catching the sizeable back draught of the distinctive Merlin engines as they kick into life on one of Britain's few remaining Lancaster bombers.

Now these are all, admittedly, rather large in nature and far from everyday occurrences. And of course, they are radio specific. But it is the principle that is important here because the basis of all this is transferable to the classroom. Every day sounds can be just as evocative. If I want to record a piece with a local retailer for business studies or maybe the town mayor for citizenship, then let's record them in the High Street. Why find the quietest room available when we can use the everyday sounds around us to help tell the story?

So back to the retailer for a moment. We want to talk about the threat from out-of-town shopping developments on a market town or family store. Then why not take our portable recorder and record then in the street with the traffic noise behind, then walk into the shop explaining what we see and get the interviewee to describe what it is they believe they can offer the shopper. There will be a difference in background sound from one location to the next, the quality of voices will switch from competing with a noisy street scene to the quieter shop. There are other sounds waiting for us – the bleeping tills, coat hangers pushed along a rack, ringing phones, an eavesdrop conversation with a customer. They all help to involve us in where we are. The advantages are pretty clear. The end result has far more impact, the sounds will not go out of date so the resource has as long a shelf life as you wish, and a recording like this need take only a fraction longer than a simple interview in that quiet room.

Editing and mixing a more complicated piece involving such additional in store sounds (see Chapter Three) but recording the conversation between the street scene and into the shop is no different to recording in a room, and it can be edited quite simply. The only difference is that the streetscape version will hold a student's attention far longer and the teacher will be far happier using it, not once, but again and again. It's a matter of confidence. This is not difficult to do, as with so many things, it is the first occasion that seems awkward and potentially clichéd. Avoid lengthy head-to-head recordings – two people asking and answering questions – if at all possible. It is dull and we switch off, mentally or otherwise.

# Epilogue

All those who have contributed to these case studies have at least something in common: they have all used audio with considerable success. They are from different backgrounds, and in some cases different countries, and have approached challenges from a differing point of view. Actually, they do share at least one other train of thought. They have all realized that audio is a credible solution, that it is fast turnaround, cost-effective and connects students and the community almost regardless of the age of the recipient. They also understand that the skills needed, to at least make a start and record something that sounds as it should, are basic. What is important is imagination and a dash of creativity.

Just pick up a recorder, press the record button and see where it takes you.

# Index